Valode & Pistre

Valode & Pistre

Complete Works: 1980 to Present

Philip Jodidio

Contents

7	The Correct Choice of Means *Philip Jodidio*	146	Shenyang Culture Hub
		148	Shimao Tower
		150	L'Ilo
20	Belier Foundry	152	Promenade Sainte-Catherine
22	Thomson LGT Factory	156	Clarins Headquarters
24	Bull Group Research Center	158	Beirut Souks
26	CAPC Bordeaux Contemporary Art Museum	162	Campus Sanofi
32	Shell Headquarters	166	Mohammed VI Exhibition Center
36	L'Oréal Factory	168	Laennec Rive Gauche
42	Leonardo da Vinci University	170	Incity Tower
46	Air France Headquarters	176	Airbus Group Leadership University
48	Renault Technocentre, La Ruche	182	Damac Tower
52	Johnson & Johnson Headquarters	184	BioMérieux Headquarters
54	Paris Expo, Pavilion 4	190	Gonesse Hospital
56	UGC Ciné-Cité Bercy	192	University of Toulouse—Jean Jaurès
60	UGC Ciné-Cité Strasbourg	198	Regional Judiciary Police Department
62	Bretonneau Hospital	200	Paris Convention Centre, Pavilion 7
64	Bercy Village	204	Shenzhen Hospital
70	Triangle de l'Arche	206	Skolkovo Innovation Center
72	Valeo Generic Factories	210	Shenzhen Exhibition Center
74	ZB4—The Wilo Building	216	Paris Expo, Pavilion 6
76	Capgemini University	220	Saint-Gobain Tower
80	Transpac	226	ABC (Autonomous Building for Citizens)
82	Renault Technocentre, Le Gradient	228	Prado Concorde
84	Paris Expo, Pavilion 5	232	Urban Garden
86	Initial Tower	234	Bulgari Hotel
90	Havas Advertising Headquarters	236	Montrouge Academy
94	Crystal Park	238	Issy—Cœur de Ville
98	Opus 12 Tower	244	Hendrikhof Tilburg
102	Las Mercedes	246	Les Ardoines Station (Grand Paris Express Station)
106	L'Oréal Laboratories		
110	Biopark Technology Center	248	Vert de Maisons Station (Grand Paris Express Station)
114	T1 Tower—Engie Headquarters		
120	Hyatt Hotel Yekaterinburg	250	Pont de Rungis Station (Grand Paris Express Station)
124	Cinetic		
128	Bouygues Technopole	252	Monaco Sea Extension
132	Lorient Hospital	258	Gare du Nord
136	Lille Main Stadium	266	Jeddah City Mall
140	Beaugrenelle Paris		
		270	Index

Jean Pistre (left) and Denis Valode (right), founders of Valode & Pistre, and the nine associates

Nicolas Bonnange [1] (HR, Finances)

Yannick Denis [2] (Architect)

Elena Fernandez [3] (Architect)

Stéphane Ferrier [4] (Development)

Valérie Poli [5] (Interior Design)

Benoît Rivet [6] (Architect)

Guohong Song [7] (Architect)

Caroline Valode [8] (Communication)

Mathew Wiggett [9] (Architect)

The Correct Choice of Means

Philip Jodidio

Valode & Pistre seem atypical in the world of contemporary architecture. Their bright, cheerful offices on the Rue du Bac in the heart of Paris reflect this nature. It seems quite natural that artists who work with light such as Yann Kersalé and the late François Morellet have been pleased to create installations specifically for these offices because, from their first iconic completed work, the renovation of the CAPC Bordeaux Contemporary Art Museum, the pair have been actively interested in the connections between art and architecture.

Built in 1824 near the River Garonne, close to the center of Bordeaux, the Entrepôt Lainé was intended to stock spices, chocolate, and vanilla coming from the French colonies. Built of brick, Bourg stone, and Oregon red pine, it was an intentionally heavy and dark structure, meant to protect its contents from the heat and light of the sun. The warehouse was not an obvious choice for the exhibition of contemporary art. Perhaps one of the most significant aspects of the intervention of Valode & Pistre on the Entrepôt Lainé is, in fact, respect for the existing building. Today, Denis Valode insists on the rather prescient interest of the office in restructuring and renovating existing buildings. As he says, "With the interest today in embodied carbon and other elements related to demolition and construction, it has almost become a crime to raze an existing structure to rebuild on the same site." While they could have made a case for a much more apparent intervention and attempted to erase all traces of the past inside this old structure, they chose not only to live with what was there, but to bring it forward so that visitors could experience something that no completely modern building can transmit—a sense of time.

A concept of architecture that is closely in keeping with the needs of the present and foreseeable future is the sense of economy that is apparent in many of their projects. As Denis Valode says, "We are convinced that the role of the architect is to do more with less and not the contrary. The economy of means—the correct choice of means—is essential. Our goal is to create the best possible result with a certain frugality of means." Once again, this interest in obtaining the maximum result with a minimum of means leads the architects to note that their approach is particularly well suited to current ecological concerns.

Denis Valode and Jean Pistre's sense of efficiency has proven to be far more durable and better adapted to the demands of contemporary architecture than the many flamboyant styles that have come and gone since they started working together. Their words are in perfect harmony with their ideas—they avoid excessive rhetoric but when they talk about buildings they do so with passion and with clear ideas and methods, often involving their aesthetic sense developed through the world of art. In 2022, Denis Valode wrote a treatise on geometry that clearly explains that the work of the office is always based on simple, Euclidean geometry and forms. He states, "Even work such as our L'Oréal Factory, which might seem to have been conceived using digital design techniques, is the result of perfectly defined and combined geometric forms. In physical science, it is coincidentally being discovered progressively that a combination of relatively simple molecules can produce much more stable and durable shapes and substances. Computer-generated forms may appear to be scientific, but they are not. In fact, some forms developed using digital tools are very difficult to master in actual construction, and we are convinced that relatively simple forms have qualities such as symmetry. This permits us to develop projects that are very clear. We do not shy away from the kind of complexity that is born of interconnecting and reiterated geometric elements on the other hand."

Denis Valode and Jean Pistre oversee one of the most successful architectural offices in France, working on prestigious towers, hospitals, and research facilities, but also on shopping centers and sports venues. Nor are their projects limited to France—they have worked in China, Russia, and numerous other countries. The pair first worked together in 1978 and created Valode & Pistre in 1980. Today the office employs 200 people and provides interior, architectural, and urban design as well as engineering services. These projects highlight the success of the office in breaking through the barriers that usually separate architects who work on privately funded projects and public ones in France.

The attachment of Valode & Pistre to Euclidean solids and variations on that theme define what underlies their work, but this style is not readily apparent in their structures because of the time and effort put into making each building correspond to its setting and to its use. Their work is modern, but not modernist in the sense that they willingly appropriate or renovate existing structures and always respond to context. Quite far removed from the *tabula rasa* of Bauhaus modernism, Valode & Pistre have actively sought out links between their projects and science, ethnology, art, sociology, or history. Jean Pistre states, "We have always tried to create a synthesis—the office is pluridisciplinary. We have specialists in ecology, structure, building skins, and other areas and this corresponds to a philosophy that is particularly well suited to taking on increasingly complex projects."

A recent example of their approach can be seen in the ABC residence in Grenoble, a sustainable apartment complex, which is the first autonomous housing structure in France. "We have been working on this project for over six years," explains Denis Valode. "We understood some time ago that although emphasis has been placed on networks in information and architecture, it is in fact the network that consumes the most energy. Our solution is to go in the opposite direction, toward capturing water and the sun rather than ejecting or avoiding them. We aim to create a building that is truly autonomous in water, energy, and waste treatment." In this case, working closely with Bouygues Construction, they achieved a 40 percent reduction in household waste, a two-thirds reduction in use of city water, and a 70 percent saving in energy use. Logically, A stands for *autonomous*, B for *building* and C for *citizens*. The social aspect of architecture is another affirmed direction in the work of Valode & Pistre.

Rather than an isolated object, a building by Valode & Pistre is conceived as being part of a tissue of relationships and situations. They examine location, activity, and history and then propose solutions that may be very unexpected but remain the fruit of their analysis of the precise situation involved. In their efficiency and affirmed modernity—in the best sense of the word—Denis Valode and Jean Pistre together with their team have staked out a considerable place in contemporary architecture, not only in France, but on the international scene as well. Denis Valode concludes, "We have defined a certain number of themes and methods that position us vis-à-vis the subjects that are essential in today's architecture. We seek maximum effect with minimum means—an approach that corresponds very directly to the needs and demands of today's ecological architecture. Our long-standing development of the idea of creating a synthesis between different areas ranging from engineering to art, makes the office thoroughly interdisciplinary, it makes us capable of handling large, complex projects across the world."

—Philip Jodidio
Lausanne, Switzerland, May 2022

Complete Works:
1980 to Present

1980 Belier Foundry

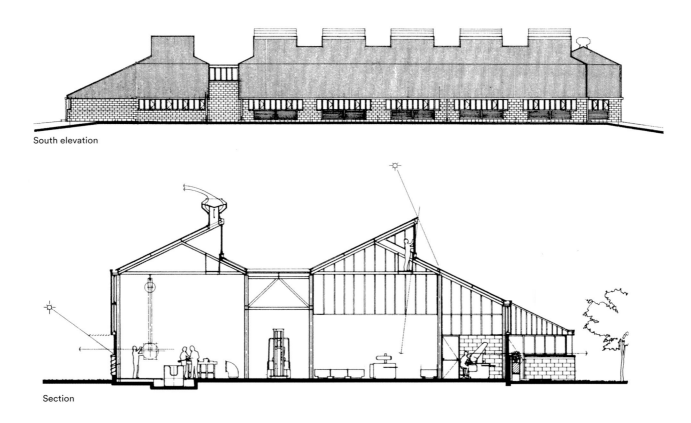

South elevation

Section

Location Vérac, France
Client Fonderie et Ateliers du Bélier
Area 12,900 ft² (1,200 m²)
Photography Valode & Pistre

The Belier Foundry project was carried out in the framework of an industrial design competition organized by the *French Agence Nationale pour L'Amélioration des Conditions de Travail* and won by Valode & Pistre.

The aim of the competition was to help develop new architectural design methods for factories. The extension of the Belier Foundry, a foundry for copper and aluminum car parts in Vérac near Bordeaux, was an opportunity to develop a multidisciplinary design approach involving not only architects, engineers, sociologists, and ergonomists but also to use input from foundry staff and management.

This was a real laboratory project aimed at building a 10,764-square-foot (1,000-square-meter) extension, involving research, iterative fine-tuning, tests using models, full-scale trials, technical measurements, and also a series of interviews, discussions, and workshops.

The process made it possible to develop a project in which architecture provides an overall response to industrial and human issues. The massing of the building, which is comprised of a combination of pitched elements, juxtaposes the production zones and the locker rooms and canteen so that the foundry blends into the landscape, much like the local wineries.

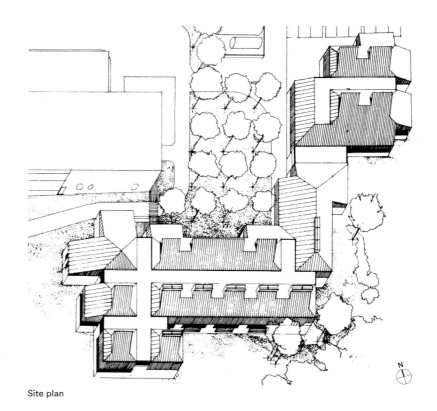

Site plan

1985 Thomson LGT Factory

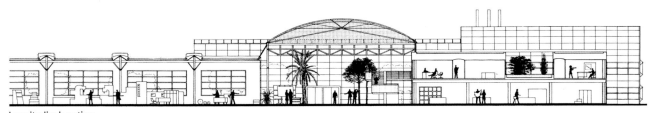
Longitudinal section

West elevation

Location Conflans-Sainte-Honorine, France
Client Thomson LGT
Area 247,500 ft² (23,000 m²)
Photography Valode & Pistre

Conflans Sainte-Honorine is located 15 miles (24 kilometers) northwest of Paris. This facility combines research and production and sales offices for Thomson LGT, a maker of telecommunications equipment. The basic form used is a square, crossed by a stretched, 'vaulted nave' where a library, café, and exhibition area are located. This is the space that brings everyone working in the complex together.

"For the Thomson LGT Factory project," Jean Pistre explains, "our work with the engineer Peter Rice began with word association, finding their keyword for the design process; as it turned out, it was the word 'point.'"

The façades are in carefully crafted glass and aluminum, completing an image of architectural precision and modernity that is confirmed by the technically sophisticated nave roof.

The architects say that the Thomson LGT Factory is a response to an industrial question—it offers spaces that are well adapted to the work and communication necessary for the specific activity of the firm and provides added value insofar as the very image of the company is concerned.

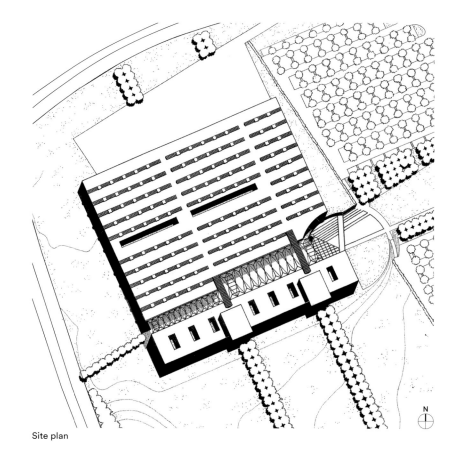
Site plan

1989 Bull Group Research Center

Hall perspective

Location Paris, France
Client AGF
Area 226,000 ft² (21,000 m²)
Photography Christophe Demonfaucon

The architects sought both to insert this building into an urban environment, but also to create a place for researchers in the city.

Located on the Avenue Gambetta in an old industrial area of Paris, this center takes up where a 1950s building leaves off, using its form and alignments to create a seamless link between the past and the present. Where the two meet the entry opens onto an old courtyard, transformed into an atrium where employees can gather and exchange ideas. An elevator tower links walkways that serve the different parts of the building. A folded fan-like shape alternates cloth and glass surfaces that modulate daylight in the atrium area.

As was the case for the Thomson LGT factory, the architects worked with the noted engineer Peter Rice for this project. A public space was created along one façade, but the atrium is an essential element in this design, connecting the old and the new with a light-flooded modern space that has proven fully conducive to the exchange of ideas among users and for work efficiency.

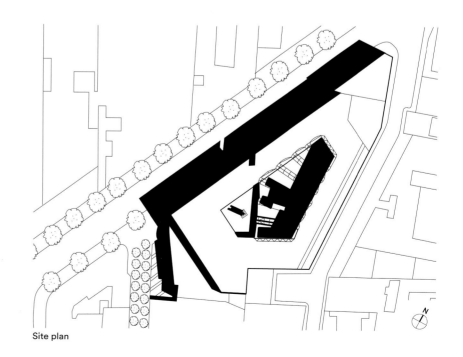

Site plan

1990 CAPC
Bordeaux Contemporary Art Museum

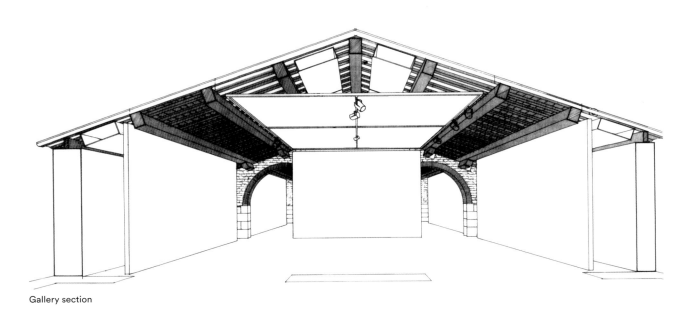

Gallery section

Location Bordeaux, France
Client City of Bordeaux
Area 161,500 ft² (15,000 m²)
Photography Alain Goustard

In Bordeaux, the rehabilitation of the 'Entrepôt Lainé' warehouse combined two objectives: a reflection on modern art, its context, and its environment; and a reflection on creating architecture through the rehabilitation of an exceptional building.

Constructed in 1824 on the left bank of the Garonne River, the 'Entrepôt' served as bonded warehousing for spices, chocolate, and vanilla shipped from overseas. Its architecture was founded in rigor and in the simple elegance of mastered geometry generated by an ingenious structural system, rather than in ornament. Heavy masonry, in stone and brick, protected the precious merchandise from the sun, creating an architecture of obscurity highlighted by rare shafts of light falling through its spaces.

Contrary to the effect of sedimentation, where each new layer masks the previous one, the restoration conserves the traces of the past: graffiti daubed by workers on stone walls, black grime accumulated on certain façades. These are measures of activity, and of time.

Reflecting an authenticity of approach, the contemporary renovation is introduced with a profound understanding and respect for this architecture of warm brick and gray limestone. White horizontal and vertical planes capture portions of space, at the same time revealing the space in which they are confined. Architecture of the past and present overlap. Contemporary museum architecture was created within that of the restored warehouse; each is independent, one reinforcing the other.

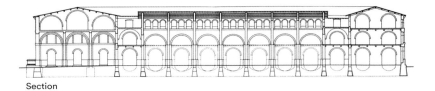

Section

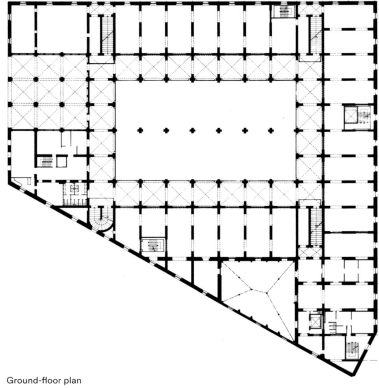

Ground-floor plan

1991 Shell Headquarters

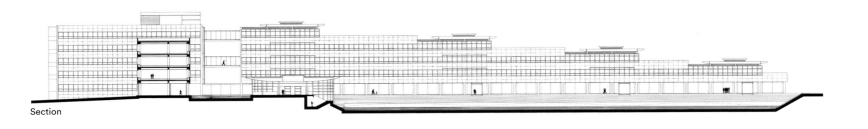
Section

North elevation

Location Rueil Malmaison, France
Client Shell France
Area 376,700 ft² (35,000 m²)
Photography Christophe Demonfaucon

The headquarters of Shell France has left the Rue Berry in Paris for the 'countryside.' In this suburban zone, the problem was no longer one of fitting in, but of composing, creating a site for Shell France in its entirety. Valode & Pistre sought to define a place, to construct not only the building, but also the site, offering spaces and gardens for a new quality of life. The building, extending to the site's limits, was designed in a spirit of fragmentation and articulation of volumes.

Facing the Chatou hills, with the River Seine flowing by below, the site is adapted to the slope it occupies. The buildings increase in height as they recede from the river bank, offering views of the Seine and the opposite bank.

Between the car park and offices, between the river and hills, under a sloping glazed roof, a gallery was created that gives access to places of rest and relaxation. With its interior street bordering a pond of water lilies, its alternation of gardens and offices, and its composition with the Chatou hills, the Shell headquarters has as much to do with landscape as it does with architecture.

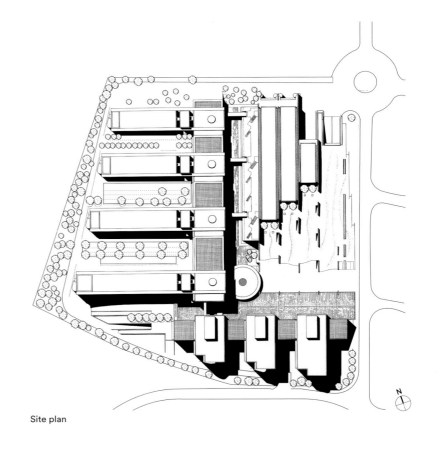
Site plan

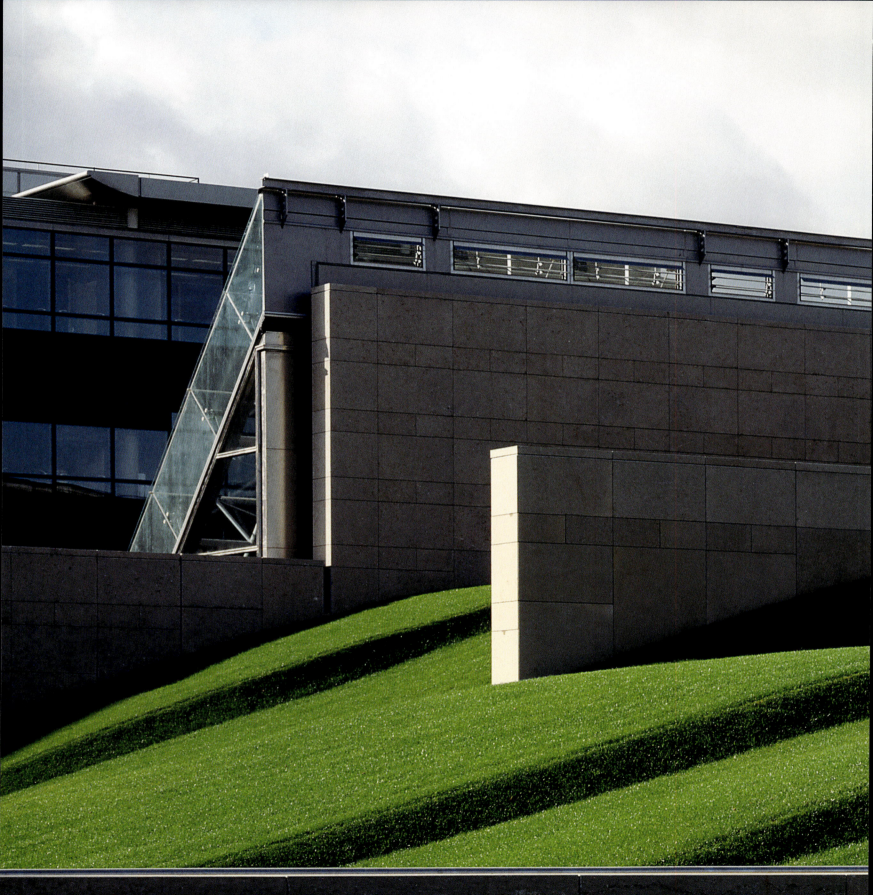

1992 L'Oréal Factory

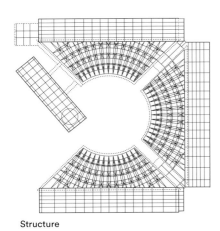
Structure

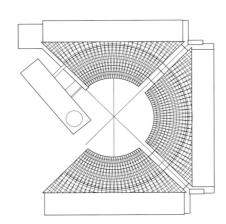

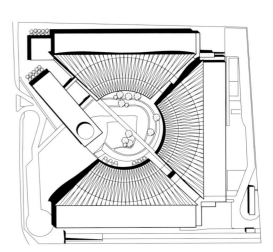

Location Aulnay-sous-Bois, France
Client L'Oréal
Area 355,200 ft² (33,000 m²)
Photography Georges Fessy, Philippe Decros, Fernando Uquijo

On the one hand, this project involves a production center geared for new industrial practices and, on the other hand, it contains a factory-scale showroom visited by thousands. The L'Oréal factory at Aulnay-sous-Bois plays a double role, providing optimal conditions for those working there and for visitors. Together, these two aspects constitute the L'Oréal image. The duality of the function conceived in formal, or even social terms, becomes a new way of considering industrial space.

With its white corolla and green center, the complex spreads its three white petals, creating a subtle marriage between poetry and geometry. The complex torus shape encloses an interior world, a perfumed garden.

Each petal corresponds to a production unit, a space free of intervening structural elements but for all that, avoiding uniformity. Light penetrates directly and abundantly, creating shadows and reflections. The variation in height, due to the roof's undulation, differentiates the packing zone looking onto the garden, from the zones devoted to preparation and production that require greater ceiling height. The three zones are independent. Suspended at mid-height above them is an overhead walkway that also encompasses the interior garden.

At Aulnay-sous-Bois, the L'Oréal factory is a manifest resolution of functional, formal, and structural constraints: its architecture uses geometry to give poetic expression to the workplace, qualities recognized by the Equerre d'argent prize given to the project in 1992.

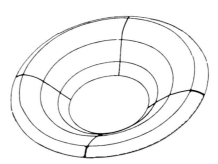

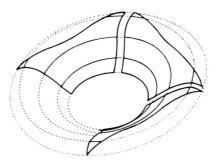

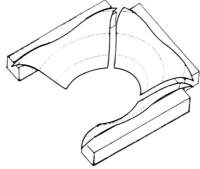
Volumetric concept

1994 Leonardo da Vinci University

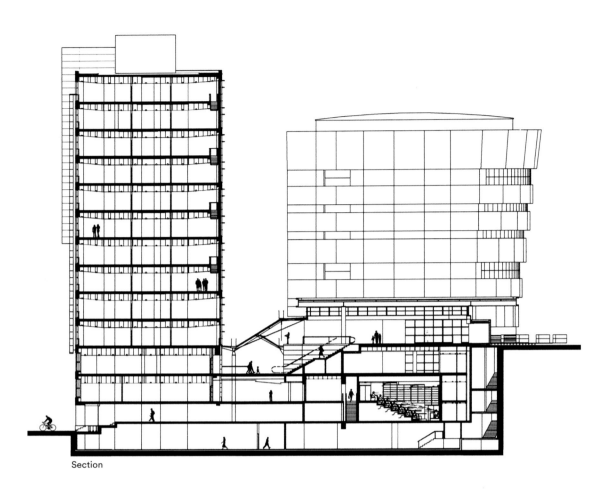

Section

Location Courbevoie, France
Client Conseil général des Hauts-de-Seine
Area 592,000 ft² (55,000 m²)
Photography Georges Fessy, Alexeï Naroditsky

In the context of the La Défense business area, the Leonardo da Vinci University, asserts its intellectual and cultural singularity.

Three elegant freestanding forms were created in front of a long, gray rectilinear building, as sculptural archetypal shapes arrayed against their background. The colors and materials accentuate the sculptural effect—the two prismatic forms, one set within the other, are of brown granite; the hollowed cube is clad in green marbled granite, and the 'prow,' an inverted cone, is covered in white marble.

This play of forms and colors corresponds to a clear functional organization: the flexible, upgradable teaching facilities are in the 'backdrop' building, and in the three freestanding edifices there are laboratories, administrative offices, and a library.

A dense, animated, well-lit interior street runs between them. The community facilities—a cafeteria, coffee bar, and gymnasiums—are located along this street, creating many opportunities for encounters between students and professors.

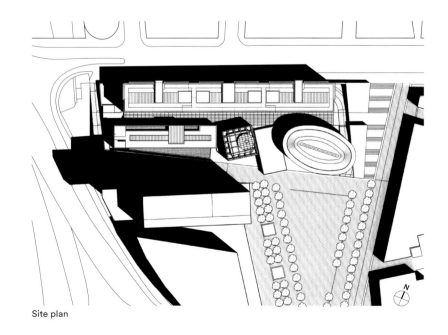

Site plan

42

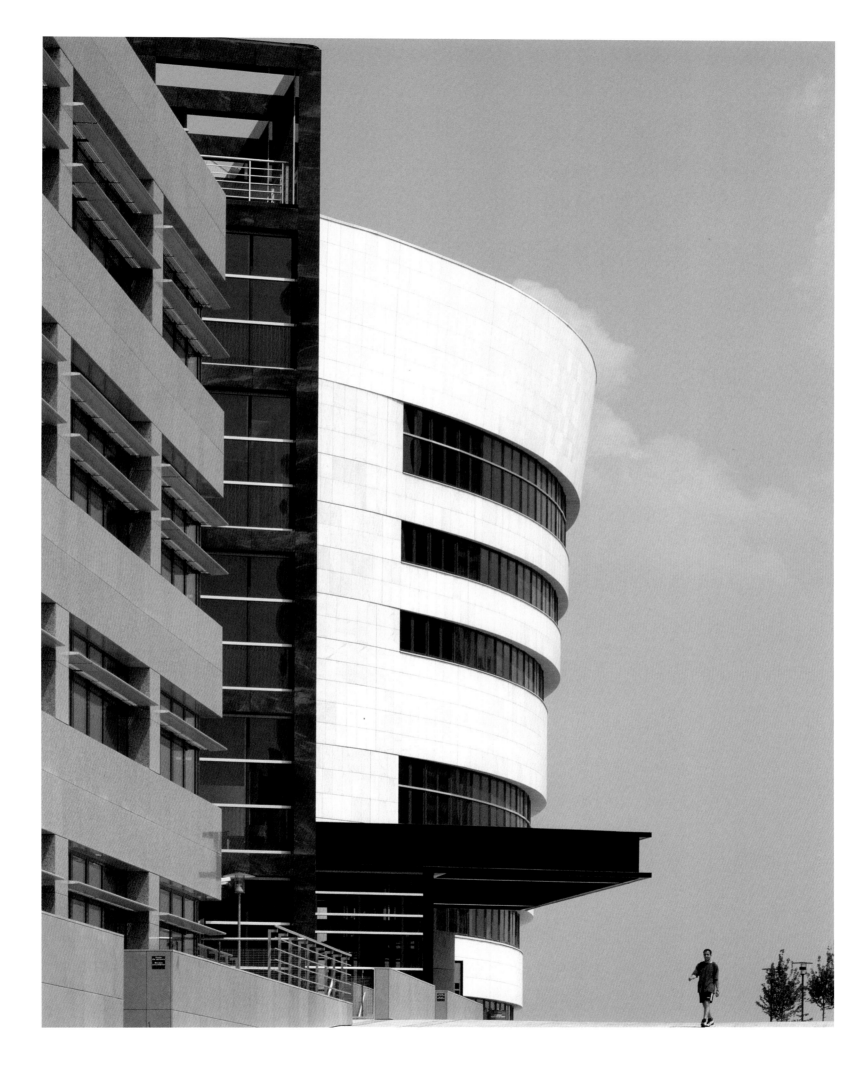

1995 Air France Headquarters

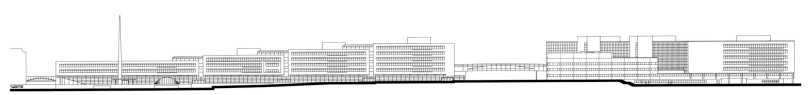
South elevation

Location Roissy, France
Client Air France
Area 1,830,000 ft² (170,000 m²)
Photography Georges Fessy

Facing the runways, visible from the boarding lounges at Roissy 2 Airport, the company headquarters of Air France and the *Cité PN* (Navigating Personnel Center) stress both dynamism and permanence.

The long white façade, rising incrementally as the floors rise, creates a tension like that of takeoff, establishing a relation with the airplanes. Set on a trapezoidal lot, the project extends to the point of occupying the site in its entirety without seeming to.

The different buildings that make it up are organized around gardens. From the square in front, three successive glazed-in volumes become visible glass towers, whose transparency reveals the depth of the site.

Above all, this is an urban layout, whose variations of scale and height establish a broader world around the individual.

The company headquarters of Air France is an architectural response to a set of complex questions, borrowing from various fields—working lifestyle, the brand image of a prestigious airline, and the constraints of a site subject to high noise levels and security—but also a poetic evocation of the aircraft, ceaselessly landing and taking off.

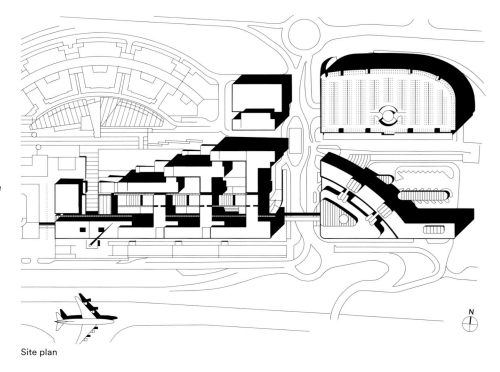
Site plan

1997 Renault Technocentre, La Ruche

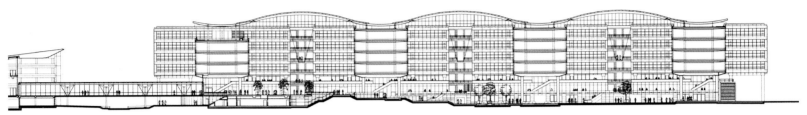

Longitudinal section

Transversal section

Location Guyancourt, France
Client Regie Nationale des Usines Renault
Area 2,475,000 ft² (230,000 m²)
Photography Georges Fessy

Located in Guyancourt, just over 12.4 miles (20 kilometers) from the center of Paris, the Ruche ('The Hive') houses the workshops and research offices of the Renault Technocentre.

It is the place where Renault vehicles are created, from fundamental and applied research to prototypes. Its complex mode of function, characterized by a great need for communication, depends on its crisscrossing network of buildings organized around planted courtyards.

Three wide atriums are in the center of the complex, covered by an immense glazed roof supported by wooden arches, forming the central core of information and meetings for the entire Technocentre. The stone and wood, allied with the glass and metal façades, underline the project's twofold dimension, contrasting and uniting the scale of the individual and the scale of the industrial group.

Valode & Pistre were also responsible for the master plan of the entire Technocentre campus.

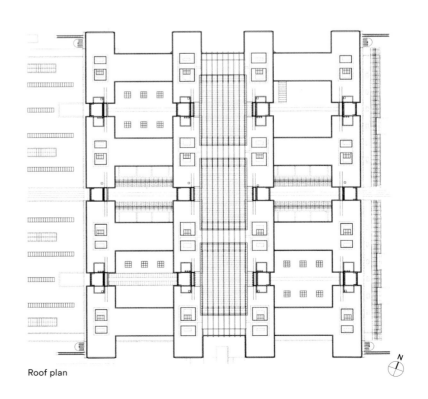

Roof plan

1997 Johnson & Johnson Headquarters

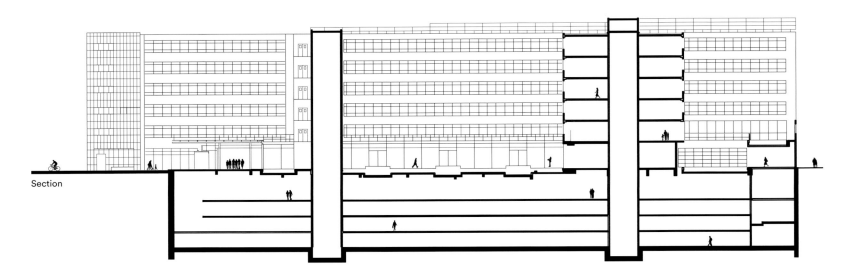
Section

Location Issy-Les-Moulineaux, France
Client Bouygues Immobilier
Area 204,500 ft² (19,000 m²)
Photography Georges Fessy

This project groups French affiliates with the American company Johnson & Johnson under one roof. Adhering to street alignments, the French Johnson & Johnson headquarters offers the city a carefully designed urban corner with restrained façades that are imbued with a feeling of quality.

The Johnson & Johnson universe, where people move, communicate and work, is developed within an envelope of urban architecture. Two long parallel buildings of unequal width face each other with a welcoming interior space occupying the area between them. The interior façades are entirely smooth, composed of alternating glazed and enameled panels. Viewed from the entirely transparent entrance hall, the interior space reveals itself in depth.

White Pennsylvanian granite, aluminum, and glass are the materials used for the Johnson & Johnson headquarters, chosen because they are both sober and durable. Employed without ostentation, they express the sophistication and delicacy associated with the healthcare community.

The company's specific nature and the image it wishes to project were, perhaps more than elsewhere, a source of the architectural inspiration and expression.

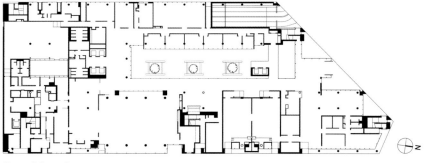
Ground-floor plan

1998 Paris Expo, Pavilion 4

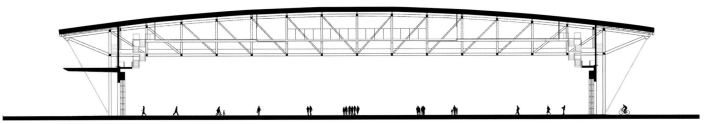

Transversal section

Location Paris, France
Client Viparis
Area 215,280 ft² (20,000 m²)
Photography Georges Fessy

Pavilion 4 is the first stage in the vast plan to restructure the Parc des Expositions at the Porte de Versailles Paris Expo site. It is designed to be a facility of exceptional dimensions: 820 feet (250 meters) long by 275.5 feet (84 meters) wide, with a clear interior height of 34.4 feet (10.50 meters).

Technical spaces in the ceilings—like those in a theater—as well as in the basements, make the various networks available throughout the building, providing for total flexibility of use. Giant beams span the 275.5-foot (84-meter) width of the building, freeing the interior space from supporting columns.

The entrances to the pavilion are signaled and magnified by the immense lever arms that hold the beams in tension. Associated with linear sky lighting, they mark the east–west axis and provide orientation and visual ease within the interior volume, for exhibitors as well as for the public.

Bordering on the Boulevard Périphérique (Paris beltway), the building is becoming the emblem of Viparis, which is the Paris exhibition's group founded by the Chamber of Commerce and Unibail-Rodamco.

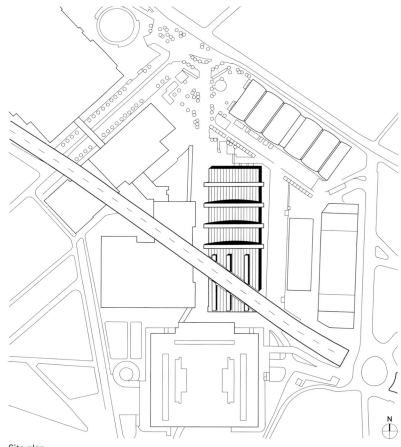

Site plan

1998 UGC Ciné-Cité Bercy

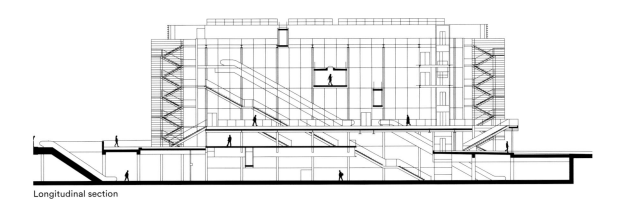

Longitudinal section

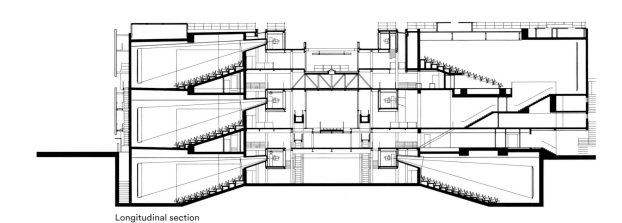

Longitudinal section

Location Paris, France
Client UGC
Area 129,000 ft² (12,000 m²)
Photography Christophe Demonfaucon

The UGC Ciné-Cité is situated in central Paris at the heart of the developing district of Bercy, near the French Ministry of Finance.

The building rises on the banks of the River Seine, prolonging the central axis of the former wine warehouses of Bercy. This area, called Bercy Village, was also renovated by Valode & Pistre.

The cinemas, clearly identifiable copper volumes, are on three levels. Channeled in from the lobby, spectators take stairs and escalators to the desired level.

The auditoriums and projection booths are connected by large cones, embodying the beam of light that projects the image onto the screen. The spectators access the cinemas from above and exit below, thus avoiding cross-floor movement.

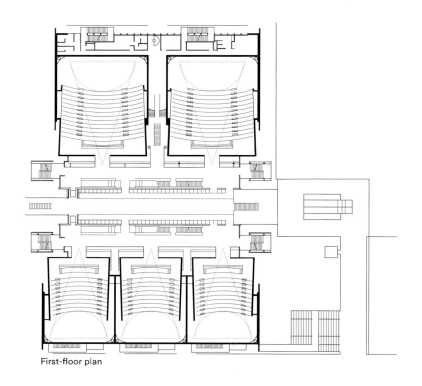

First-floor plan

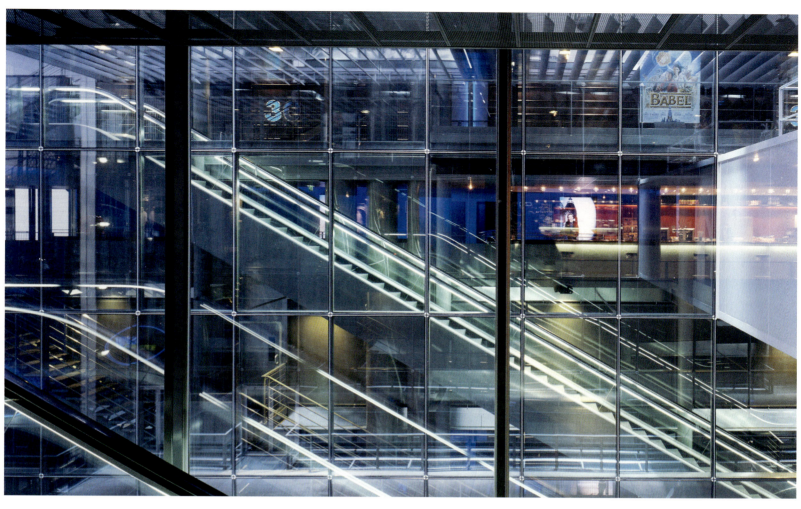

1999 UGC Ciné-Cité Strasbourg

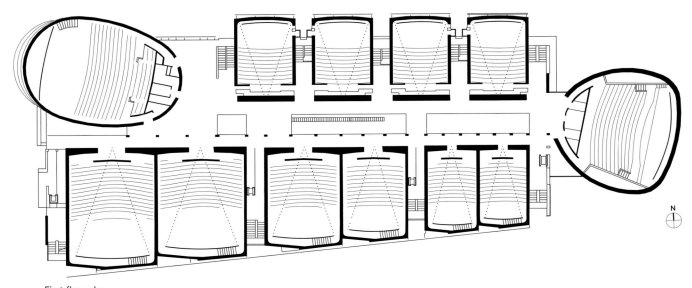

First-floor plan

Longitudinal section

Location Strasbourg, France
Client UGC
Area 183,000 ft² (17,000 m²)
Photography Christophe Demonfaucon

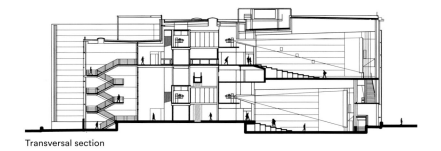

Transversal section

Between the Austerlitz basin and the RN 4 highway, the UGC Ciné-Cité Strasbourg Etoile was the first building in a new district of the eastern French city called the Fronts de Neudorf.

On one side is the traffic headed for Germany; on the other are the still waters of the Austerlitz basin, the embankment, and the pedestrians. The site stands out for this duality, and logically, the architecture is founded on this ambivalence.

In the interior, an immense lighted entry hall gives way to 'streets' on two levels. The ambiance darkens gradually as spectators reach the total darkness of the cinemas. At each end, the Ove and UGC Max rooms balance one another. Covered in green copper, they contribute to this urban landmark.

2000 Bretonneau Hospital

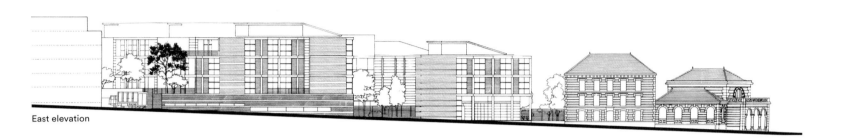
East elevation

North elevation

Location Paris, France
Client Assistance publique—Hôpitaux de Paris (AP-HP)
Area 188,500 ft² (17,500 m²)
Photography Georges Fessy

At the foot of the hill of Montmartre, the 188,500-square-foot (17,500-square-meter) Bretonneau Geriatric Hospital built for the public health service of Paris, extends out from the buildings of the original hospital. The new buildings are organized in a strict matrix, a network of built spaces articulated by quiet gardens. From one century to another, the new architecture was designed to respond to the old. In a new concept, the Bretonneau Geriatric Hospital brings elderly persons to live in Paris, in an urban place that is respectful of their intimacy. An interior street runs through it, bringing together meeting spaces. The hospitalization units are organized in the form of houses, with fifteen persons living in each pavilion. The forms, the materials and the fittings reconstitute a domestic universe, conceived so that the patients can feel at home, an essential element of geriatric care.

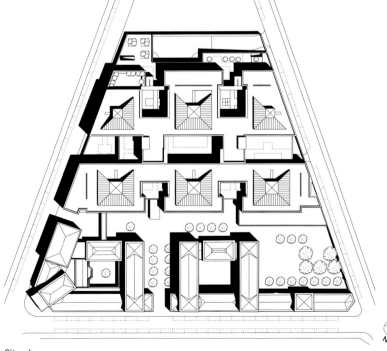
Site plan

62

2001 Bercy Village

Longitudinal section

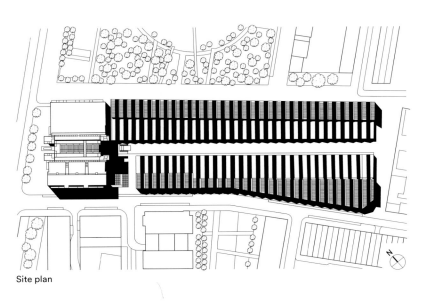
Site plan

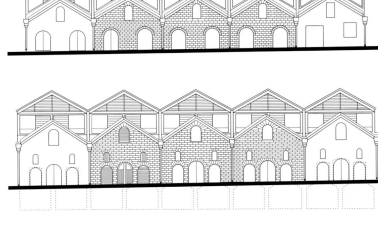

Elevations 1, 2, 3, 4: Cour Saint-Émilion; elevation 5: new façades on the park

Location Paris, France
Client SCI Bercy Village / Altarea
Area 322,900 ft² (30,000 m²)
Photography Christophe Demonfaucon, André Morin

The former wine warehouse buildings of eastern Paris, with their rough stonewalls and sloped roofs with flat brown tiles, are aligned perpendicular to the Seine River opposite the French National Library.

Boutiques, bars, and restaurants have given the place new life. On either side of the restored warehouse buildings, new ones have been built as an extension of the existing ones. Long pleated zinc roofs echo their rhythm and geometry on a larger scale. The structures are made with metal and stone fill, glazing, or wood weatherboarding.

From the small warehouse buildings of the early twentieth century to the new shops, Bercy Village takes into account time and place in a quest for authenticity.

The complex receives about fifteen million visitors per year, it's one of the most popular destinations for tourists and Parisians.

2001 Triangle de l'Arche

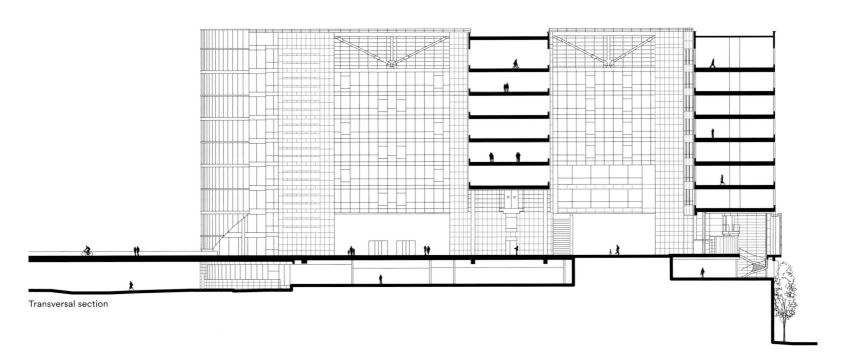

Transversal section

Location La Défense, France
Client Meunier Promotion
Area 468,500 ft² (43,500 m²)
Photography Georges Fessy

At the meeting point of two railway lines and several roadways, a triangular site was created, between the Leonardo da Vinci University and the higher ground of the Grande Arche. Resulting from a new urban vision for La Défense, the Triangle de l'Arche project proposes an urban development at a human scale, directly linked to the Grande Arche esplanade.

Governed by the surrounding road and rail networks, the buildings follow the lines of the routes. Within this environment of curves, an orthogonal urban pattern structures the site, giving this ensemble of offices the modularity and flexibility necessary for its planning.

The orthogonal system is in stone, while curvilinear elements are in glass: here and there the former breaks through the latter, exposing the building's internal nature at the periphery.

A synthesis of several currents of thought that emerged during the twentieth century, Triangle de l'Arche brings together a rediscovered urbanism at the human scale, the expression of its structural system and a thoughtful reflection on the quality of life in a new urban area.

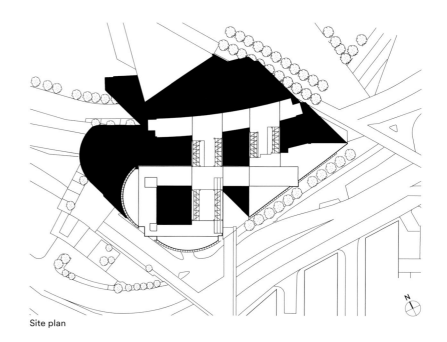

Site plan

2001 Valeo Generic Factories

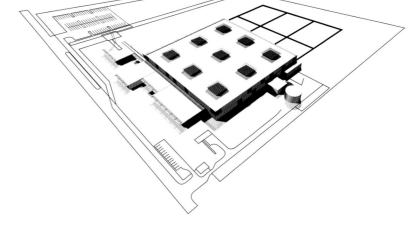

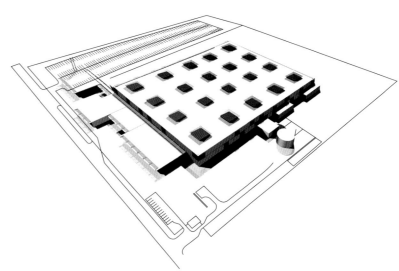

Axonometric views

Location China, Czech Republic, Hungary, Mexico, Morocco, Poland
Client Valeo
Area 108,000–247,500 ft² (10,000–23,000 m²)
Photography Valode & Pistre

Embracing a diverse range of locations, activities, and societies, Valode & Pistre have carried out theoretical and architectural research for Valeo. This research, which gave rise to a number of completed projects in Veszprem (Hungary), San Luis Potosi (Mexico), Skawina (Poland), Bouznika (Morocco), and in Wuhan (China), was called L'usine générique (The Generic Factory).

It acted as a guide, and involved defining a genre, not an object. Each entity—the factory floor, the technical elements, the offices, and services—was specially designed and combined with the others.

The vast factory floor has a skylit area at the center. Labs and engineering offices are open-space areas; their location and layout combine confidentiality and visual communication with the production area.

L'usine générique has a geographical dimension in that it involves defining constituent elements, the way they are positioned, and the way they relate to one another. This process is then updated according to the factory and the processes in question.

The factory floor, the 'satellites,' and the 'cursor' make up the overall 'map' of the factory, whose chosen site and industrial processes constitute both constraints and assets; the relevance of each unique solution depends on these three intersecting parameters.

2001 ZB4—The Wilo Building

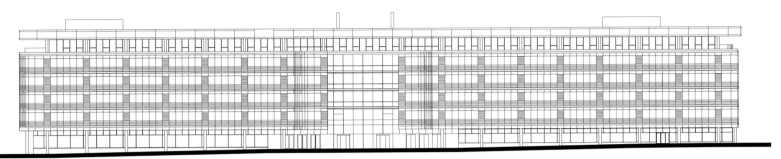

East elevation

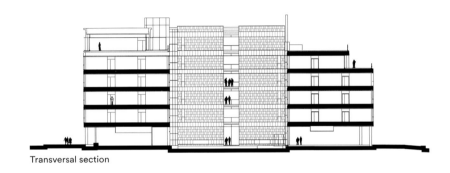

Transversal section

Location Saint-Denis, France
Client Kaufman & Broad
Area 312,000 ft² (29,000 m²)
Photography André Morin

On the plain south of Saint-Denis and at the center of a new business district, situated between the Stade de France and a railway station, the new headquarters for Generali unites various urban components comprising this quickly evolving neighborhood.

A grid of long building volumes faces François Mitterrand Avenue, with lower volumes opposite to an adjoining housing development. The complex is expressed as a series of urban events—rounded street angles, a crowning attic floor, a monumental entry porch, and interior gardens visible from the parallel streets.

With a rigorously designed interior circulation system, centered on a stone-clad core within the garden space, numerous occupancy configurations can be accommodated. Built in steel with 59-foot (18-meter) free spans and integrated building services, the flexibility of the design is evident.

The façade's dark bronze color, combined with a horizontal treatment creates a strong presence, affirming the building's urban vocation.

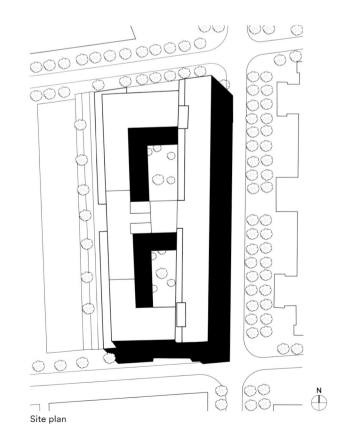

Site plan

2002 Capgemini University

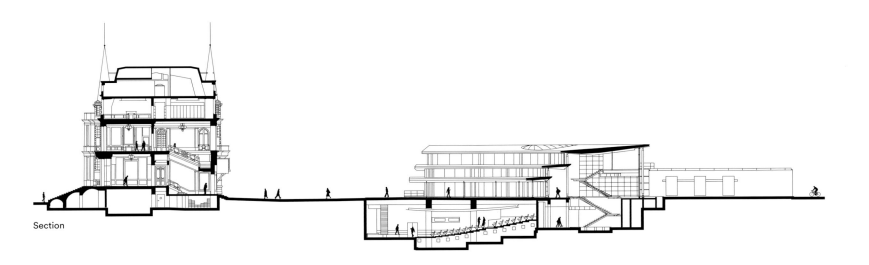

Section

Location Gouvieux, France
Client Ernst & Young
Area 247,500 ft² (23,000 m²)
Photography Benoît Fougeirol

Capgemini University, located in Gouvieux near Chantilly, is a place dedicated to corporate identity. The site comprises a large park dating from the eighteenth century and a château built by the Rothschild family.

The park has been returned to its original boundaries and the château was restored. The new campus, with its brick-and-stone buildings and concentric copper disks, is inscribed in a half-circle, centered on the main axis of the château. The campus and the château resonate together. The principal figure borrows as much from the orangerie as it does from the ancient form of the cloister.

The semi-circular space, closed by the façade of the château, creates a serene setting, freed from the contingencies of the outside world—a place for concentration and intellectual effervescence.

From the eclectic château to the resolutely contemporary campus, the quality and permanence of the architecture echo the excellence and long life that the company aspires to.

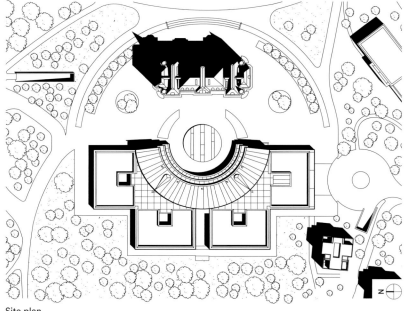

Site plan

2002 Transpac

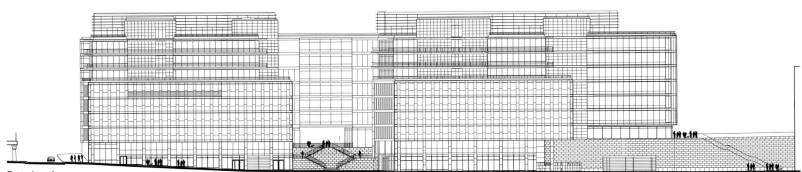

East elevation

Location Paris, France
Client Meunier Promotion
Date 2002
Area 204,500 ft² (19,000 m²)
Photography Benoît Fougeirol

Located at the intersection between Paris's new Seine Rive Gauche area and older, preserved areas, the building follows the shape of the complex site. Flanked on one side, by a broad raised avenue, on the other by a boulevard, and, overhead, by the metro, the architecture responds to a heterogeneous context of different urban situations.

Along the Avenue de France, a long glass wall, projecting a sober and contemporary image, echoes the curved shape of the lot. With its curved glass prow and glazed footbridges, the building at times allows the viewer to see completely through it.

Facing the older Paris buildings, the scale and materials of the façades provide a subtle transition between two types of construction and between two eras. At once contextual and contemporary, the building prolongs and connects the historic areas and the new district.

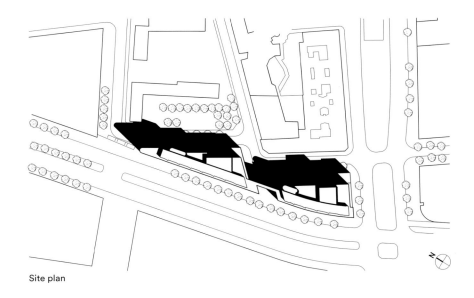

Site plan

2002 Renault Technocentre, Le Gradient

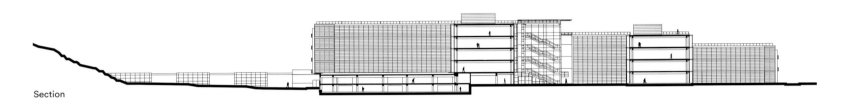
Section

Location Guyancourt, France
Client Regie Nationale des Usines Renault
Area 506,000 ft² + parking 140,000 ft²
(47,000 m² + parking 13,000 m²)
Photography Georges Fessy

The Technocentre incorporates both industrial and tertiary buildings.

Conceived as a coherent urban entity, it is encircled by a ring road. Embedded in the eastern hillside, this building is located on the edge of the site. It rises gradually, accompanying the natural slope. Governed by the existing contours, its logic is more topographic than urban. The ensemble is made up of a series of alternating patios and built volumes.

On the ground floor, open to the gardens, a long interior street crosses the building from one end to the other. Forming a central spine, it gives access on one side to the communal spaces and on the other to the vertical circulation cores and walkways. The large span structure obviates the need for intermediate columns, offering total freedom in organizing the interior.

In front of the external glazing and detached from it by continuous external walkways, blinds with broad louvers add an additional thickness to the façade. In 9.8-foot (3-meter) modules, the blinds can be drawn up or down, controlled individually or automatically. The façade, whose only apparent material is aluminum, has an appearance varies accordingly.

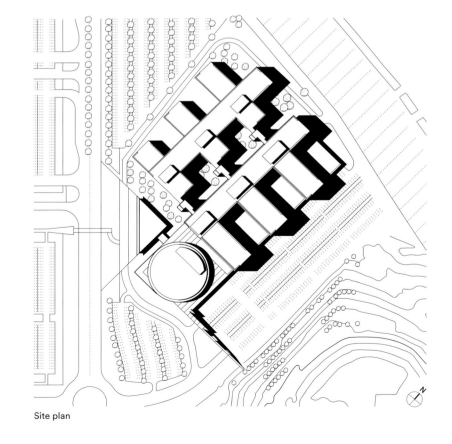
Site plan

2003 Paris Expo, Pavilion 5

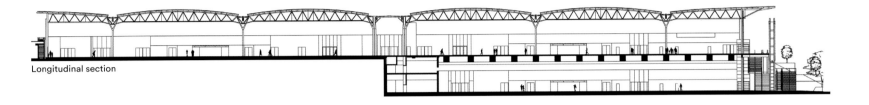
Longitudinal section

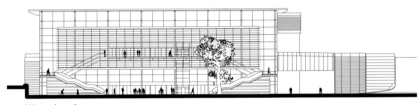
West elevation

Location Paris, France
Client Viparis
Area 245,000 ft² (22,800 m²)
Photography Georges Fessy

Located in the Parc d'Expositions de la Porte de Versailles, this building asserts its presence in the city as an urban exhibition pavilion.

To accommodate the sloping site, two pavilions were superimposed, with 230-foot-wide (70-meter-wide) floor spans and total flexibility of use. On the city side, the façade, constructed of large aluminum-clad panels and glazed curtain walls, is placed on a solid base made up of layers of polished concrete. The roof forms an undulating form on the scale of the site itself, with seven large curvilinear canopies advancing toward the boulevard.

On the esplanade in front of the pavilion, the main façade, visible from a distance, is made up of a louvered exterior screen wall that serves as a support for lighting and giant advertising panels, behind which is a transparent curtain wall opening onto the superimposed pavilions.

Monumental stairways and escalators are organized symmetrically in the space between them, forming a pronaos, leading to a belvedere with a unique view of Paris.

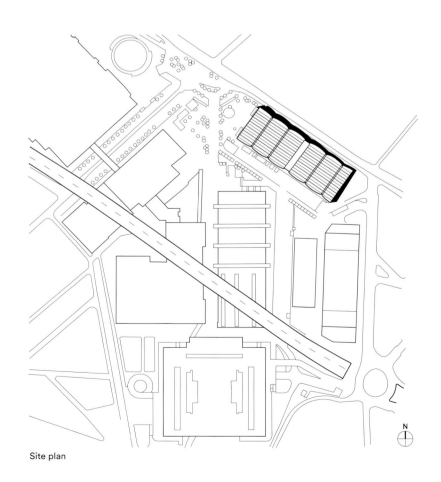
Site plan

2003 Initial Tower

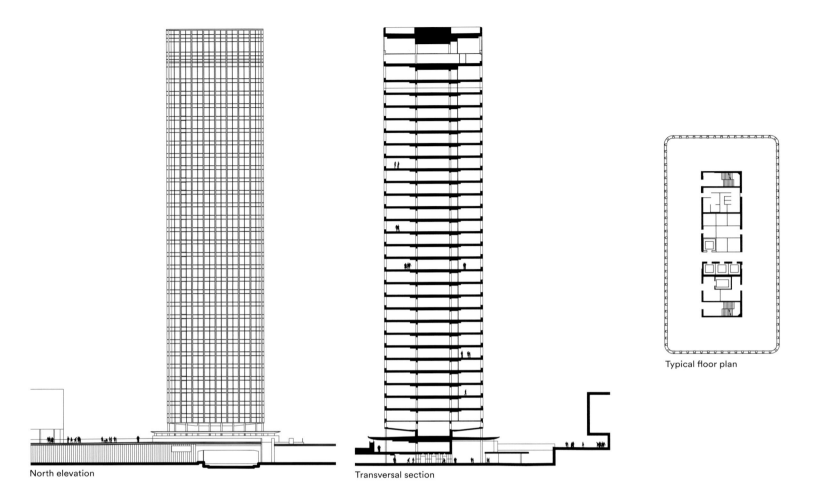

North elevation

Transversal section

Typical floor plan

Location La Défense, France
Client Tertial / Sari
Area 420,000 ft² (39,000 m²)
Photography Georges Fessy, Valode & Pistre

As its name implies, the Initial Tower was the first built at La Défense, and was designed by the noted engineer Jean Prouvé and the architects De Mailly and Depussé.

Its renovation encompassed both the restoration of the many inventive ideas presented in this architectural precursor and its introduction into the contemporary world via a reformulation of the interior spaces, with light as the principal material.

Inside, a universe of light brings the tower into line with contemporary sensibilities, without creating stylistic intrusions on the work of the original architects. Luminous ceilings, opalescent walls, and the dematerialization of opaque surfaces using planes of colored light are among the elements of the design.

In the evening, with the rows of lights set along the border of each floor slab and the central core, like a heart of light, the tower proclaims its renewal and its unique presence among the chorus of towers at La Défense.

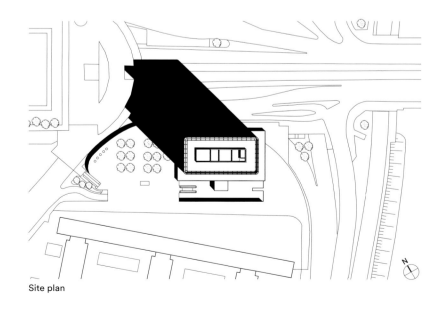

Site plan

2003 Havas Advertising Headquarters

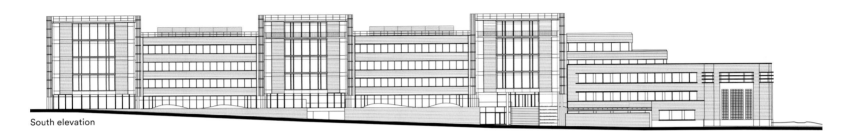

South elevation

Location Suresnes, France
Client Hines
Area 245,000 ft² (22,800 m²)
Photography Hervé Abbadie

Located on the banks of the River Seine in Suresnes outside of Paris, the building respectfully harmonizes with the former Coty perfume factory, a fine example of the architecture of the 1930s.

In a dialogue between the buildings, the task was to designate the old and the new and to reveal them. Behind the smaller-scaled brick building is a first glass screen, like a backdrop, and then the other buildings. The contemporary architecture asserts itself, without imposing its presence. Parallel to the Seine, three wings intersect with brick volumes that prolong the former factory and form an alternating sequence of buildings and gardens.

Brick, the preserved building's characteristic material, appears in variants—transversal façade bases, or fine lines embedded in the glass, making for a unified and contemporary reading of the architectural ensemble.

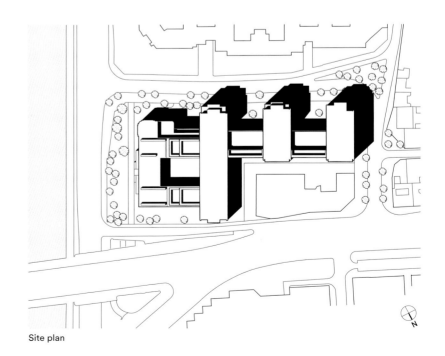

Site plan

2003 Crystal Park

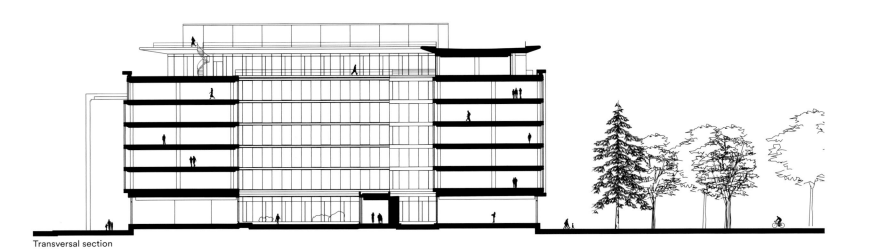

Transversal section

Location Neuilly-sur-Seine, France
Client GCI / Eiffage Immobilier
Area 495,000 ft² (46,000 m²)
Photography André Morin

Originally, this was the site of a vast group of 1960s buildings in an exceptional parkland area, once the headquarters of Saint-Gobain.

The simplification of the structure, the addition of new volumes, the reorganization of both vertical and horizontal circulation, and the redesign of the façades and the interior resulted in improved communication, flexibility, divisibility, and work conditions corresponding to the most recent user requirements in office space, which were unheard of in the past.

The glazed walls of the new 'breathing façade' look out over the parkland, seeming to frame the vegetal panorama. They create a sense of transparency and modernity, resonating with and prolonging the options of the original 1960s architecture.

In the heart of the park, an elegant pavilion—now housing a restaurant, fitness club, amphitheater, and dividable meeting rooms—was restored with care.

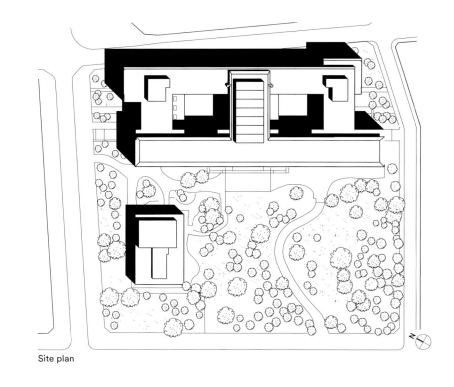

Site plan

2004 Opus 12 Tower

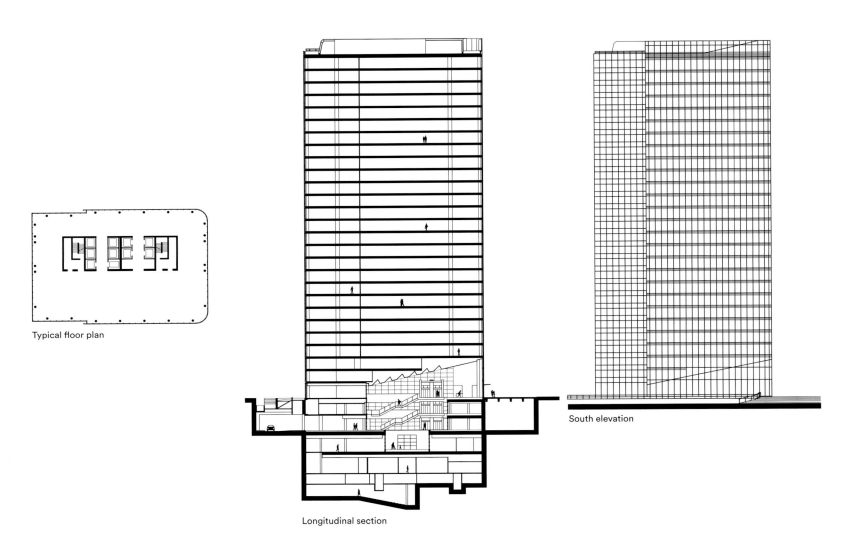

Typical floor plan

Longitudinal section

South elevation

Location La Défense, France
Client Axa / Cogedim
Area 388,000 ft² (36,000 m²)
Photography André Morin, Michel Denancé

On the southern side of the Esplanade, in the part of La Défense that is undergoing renewal, Opus 12 Tower was revamped and now stands out, thanks to its new appearance.

In place of the corncob-shaped columns that marked its façades, a lighter, more panoramic load-bearing structure was created. The resulting gain in floor area enlarged the work spaces, and the technical facilities of the tower were adapted to today's needs.

Enveloped in a double skin of clear and opalescent glass, the building takes on not only a new appearance, but also a new meaning. The high lobby opens resolutely on to the Esplanade of La Défense and also exposes the tower's infrastructure, revealing its anchoring.

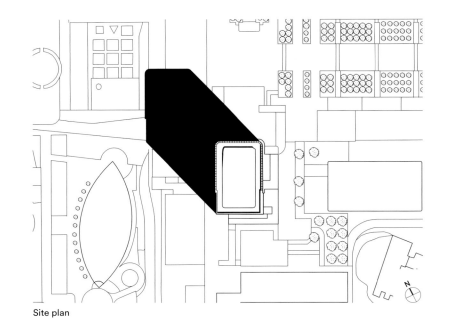

Site plan

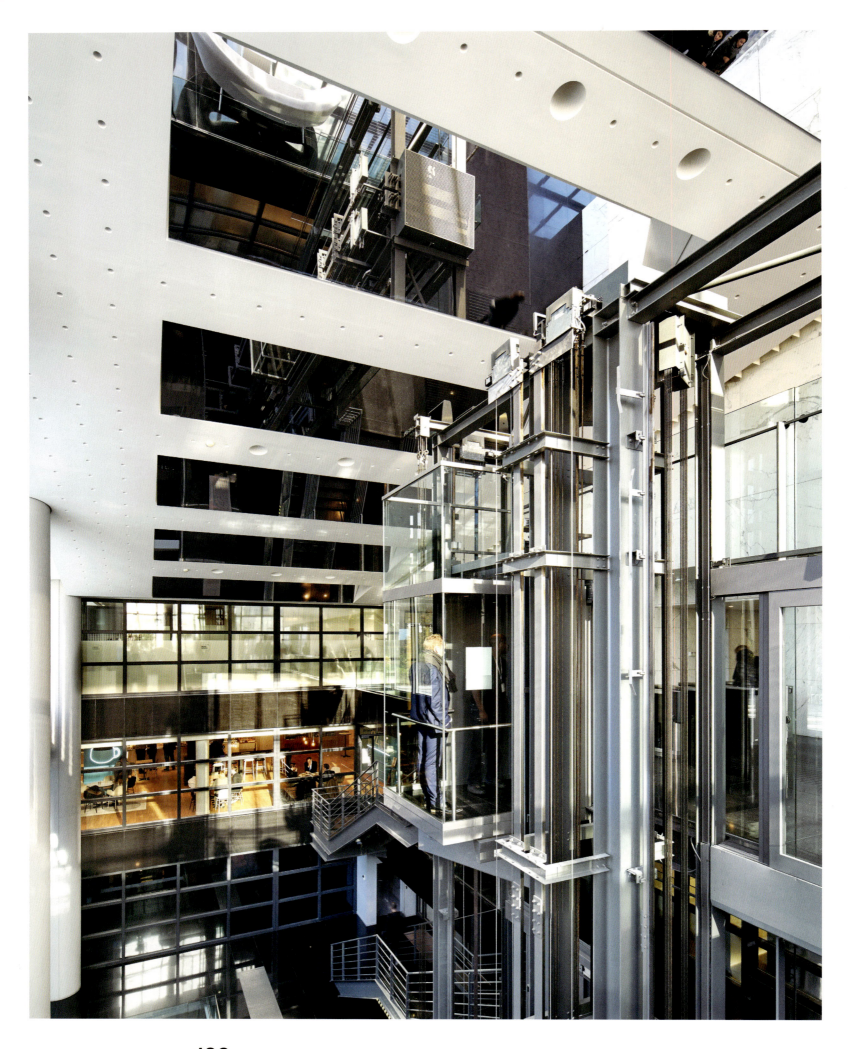

2005 Las Mercedes

South elevation

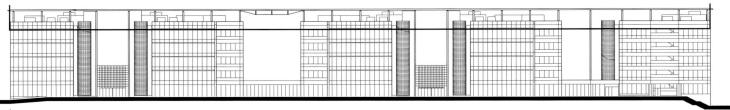

North elevation

Location Madrid, Spain
Client Nexity España / Standard Life
Area 845,000 ft² (78,500 m²)
Photography André Morin

Las Mercedes was a brown-field industrial site situated on one of Madrid's main arteries, near the airport. The new business park was conceived as an urban campus. It is urban in its use of building blocks and the creation of perimeter street walls and forms a campus due to the creation of a generous central green space.

The project's perimeter, comprising T-shaped building modules, aligns street side double façades to create an exterior 'show window.' Toward the interior, building volumes penetrate the central space providing significant façade contact with the gardens.

An entry pavilion groups together common services, crowned by a pergola linking several building volumes. The central space, sheltered from the noise of surrounding roads, is planted with tiered gardens, and includes a sunken restaurant opening on to trees and a water feature, creating a quiet and refreshing environment.

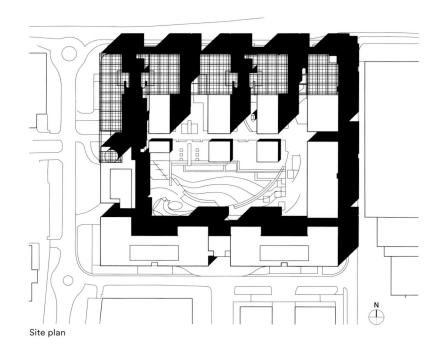

Site plan

2006 L'Oréal Laboratories

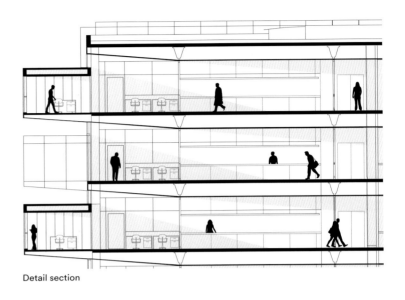

Detail section

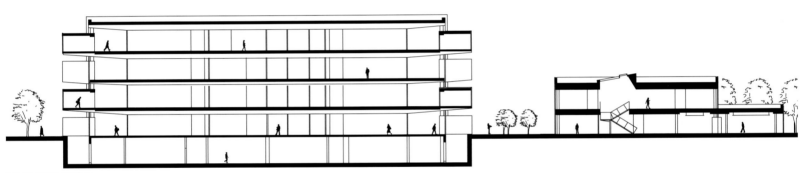

Longitudinal section

Location Chevilly-Larue, France
Client L'Oréal
Area 102,000 ft² (9,500 m²)
Photography André Morin

Located at the historic site occupied by Lancôme perfumes, 5.6 miles (9 kilometers) south of Paris, the research center is part of the Chevilly-Larue campus.

Designed like a machine, it is built on a square plan with the research spaces in the middle and the researchers' offices housed in cantilevered volumes on the façade. In these 'nests' in the sky, the scientists are at home, freed of daily cares and able to concentrate fully on their work, following the principle of domestic privacy.

The alternate play of the louvers during the day and the lighting at night complement the animation of the façades, whose interactive nature gives evidence of the activities going on within.

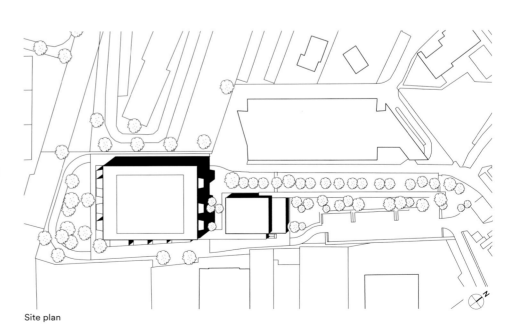

Site plan

2006 Biopark Technology Center

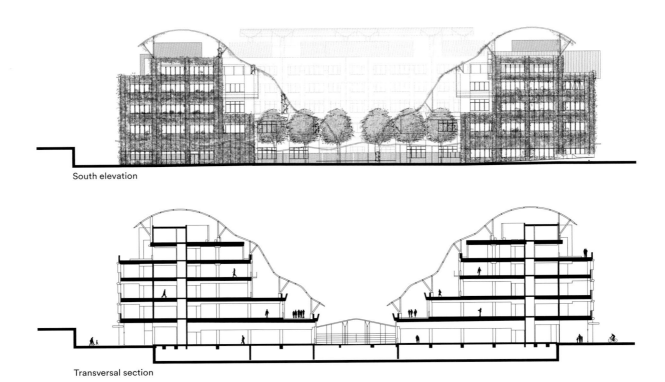

South elevation

Transversal section

Location Paris, France
Client Sagi
Area 377,000 ft² (35,000 m²)
Photography André Morin, Michel Denancé, Alexeï Naroditsky

Located in the Austerlitz development zone of eastern Paris, this design involved the updating of a 1980s complex to be used as a biotechnology center. The structure of the original, large industrial building was left unchanged, but the intervention of Valode & Pistre sought to 'reframe, restructure, and redefine' its form to better integrate it into the city and to connect it with new nearby university facilities along the banks of the Seine.

The built volumes were split to make way for a new road system that irrigates the heart of the urban block that is freed of its former slab and transformed into an open square. The cut gable ends with a metal trellis, forming a support for vegetation that, in a sense, symbolizes the change of use of the building.

Formerly austere, the heart of the block has become a green environment with its façades stepped into terraces, doubled by a generous wave-like pergola covered with roses, acanthus, and clematis. This vegetal cascade protects the offices from the otherwise strong presence of the sun. External blinds, stringcourses, and industrial boarding supplement the redesign of the façades, which takes on a new dynamism.

Working with a limited budget, the architects did not contradict the existing architecture but succeeded in bringing real breathing space into the area, in particular with the real presence of vegetation.

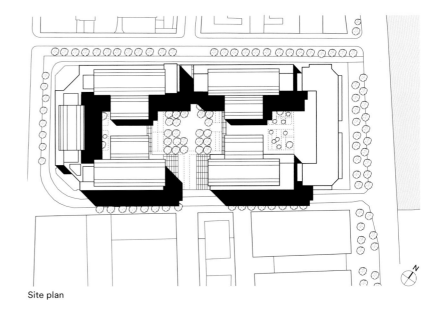

Site plan

2008 T1 Tower—Engie Headquarters

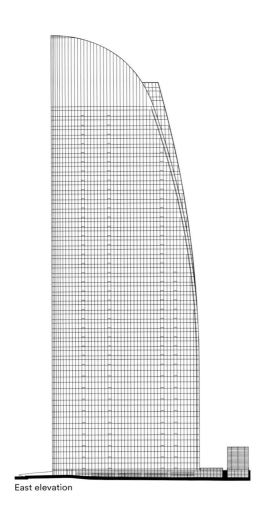
East elevation

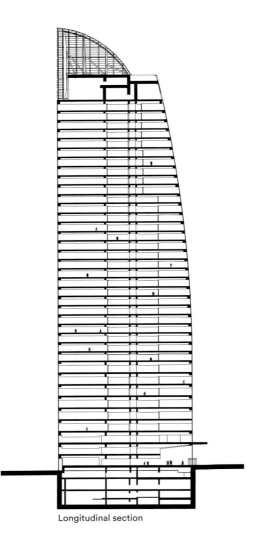
Longitudinal section

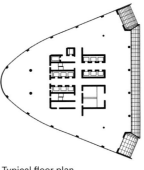
Typical floor plan

Location La Défense, France
Client Hines
Area 754,000 ft² (70,000 m²)
Photography Michel Denancé, Alexeï Naroditsky, G.D. Morand

The T1 Tower was designed as a 656-foot (200-meter) glass leaf-shaped object, folded down the south side and curving gradually on the north side. In geometric terms, this leaf is a vertical curvilinear dihedron, the base of which is part of an oval extending into two tangents forming a horseshoe. This dihedron is intersected by a large parabolic form. It is this intersection that generates the tower's morphology.

This geometric design makes it possible to design repetitive elements, the curve of the sides depending on the articulation of the joints. It produces a new form that changes according to one's viewpoint.

Seen from the south, it looks like a vertical ship's prow in harmony with the cluster of large towers at La Défense. Seen from the east and west, it looks like a huge sail with a gradual curve and asymmetrical outline that embody a transition with respect to the town below. Seen from the north, it is a large, curved ladder thrusting upwards, with the curve of the façade making it seem to vanish into the sky.

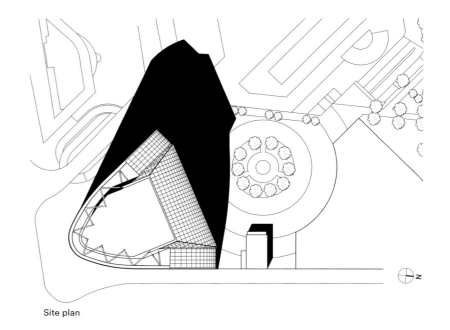
Site plan

2008 Hyatt Hotel Yekaterinburg

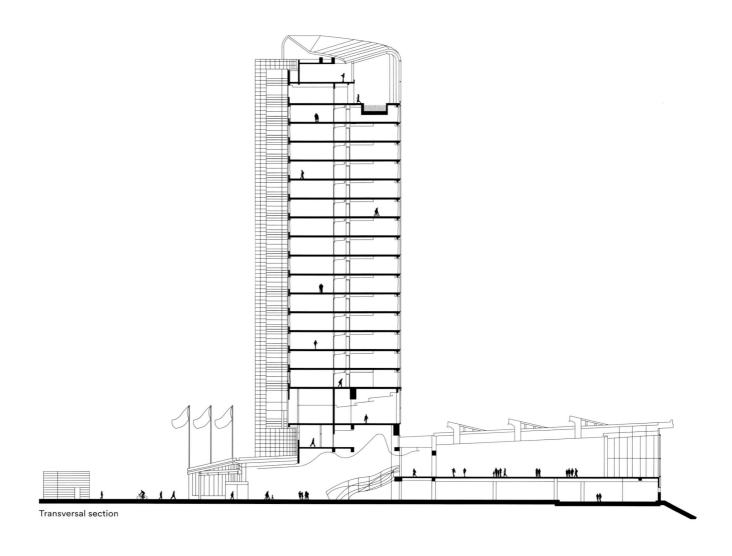

Transversal section

Location Yekaterinburg, Russia
Client UGMK / Bouygues Bâtiment International
Area 323,000 ft² (30,000 m²)
Photography Alexeï Naroditsky

This luxury hotel was the first built project of the vast Ekat City project in Yekaterinburg, Russia. The site is exceptional, located along the Iset River, and allowing the building to be aligned with the axis of the cathedral.

The hotel adopts lightness in its enveloping, protective shape. The slim, crystalline 262.4-foot (80-meter) tower offers a panorama of its surrounding environment. On the city side, a series of technological filters marry stone, copper, and glass, producing a subdued atmosphere that encourages fluid, airy interior circulation. On the riverside, a glass shield with an outward-curving profile provides the 300 rooms with total visibility of the river and the horizon beyond.

Extreme weather conditions with temperatures ranging from −31°F (−35°C) in winter up to 95°F (35°C) in summer are dealt with by the triple-glazed façade and mechanical air-flow system.

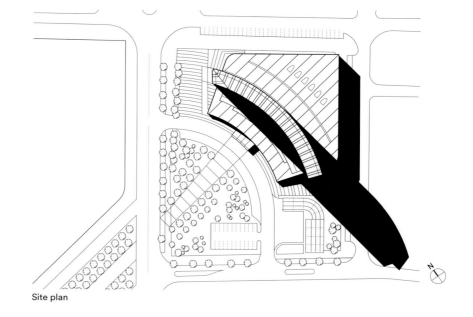

Site plan

2009 Cinetic

Concept art by Elisabeth Ballet

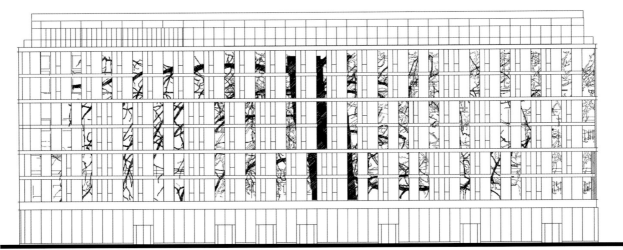

West elevation

Location Paris, France
Client Cogedim / Sogeprom / Adim
Area 237,000 ft² (22,000 m²)
Photography Michel Denancé, Alexeï Naroditsky

A strategic element in the re-qualification of Paris's Porte des Lilas, the 'Cinetic' office building respects the expected symmetry effect and assumes the role of gateway between Paris and its contiguous suburbs.

The project presents different, strongly identified façades according to the orientation and nearby buildings—in particular, the northwest façade on the Avenue de la Porte des Lilas, which stands out for its innovative, irregular folded patterns. The folds oriented to the north on the suburban side are in clear glass, and those facing west on the Paris side are in silk-screened glass, serving as the medium for a kaleidoscopic work by the artist Elisabeth Ballet, representing a close-up of a chestnut tree and its branches.

This artwork highlights the building's architectural and planning goals with sensitivity and intelligence by making them perceptible to the public.

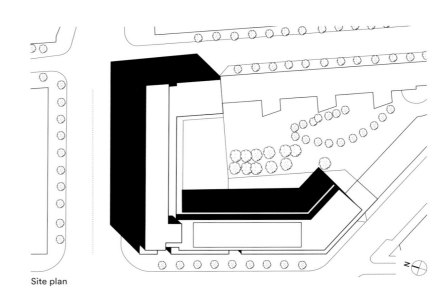

Site plan

2009 Bouygues Technopole

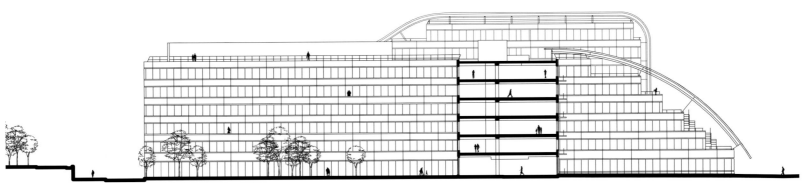
Transversal section

Location Meudon-la-Forêt, France
Client Bouygues Telecom
Area 614,000 ft² (57,000 m²)
Photography Alexeï Naroditsky

Located at the edge of the Meudon Forest near Paris, the Technopole is at once a showcase project, an exemplary site with regards to working conditions, and an environmental project.

The arrangement of the buildings, a kind of double 'V' that penetrates the forest, creates a strong relationship with the wooded environment. The gradually rising curvilinear silhouettes of the complex evoke a natural relief and culminate on the motorway side to form a signal.

The treatment of the façades is adapted to the different orientations—panoramic toward the north in the direction of the forest, diaphragmed to the east and west, and shaded to the south.

A central street opens onto gardens irrigating the building and linking the social spaces to the working environment. The continuous and flexible floor plans facilitate the establishment and the evolution of the activities of the Technopole.

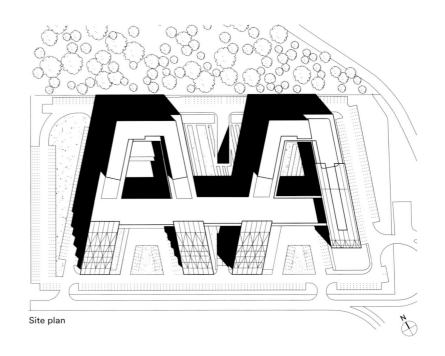
Site plan

2012 Lorient Hospital

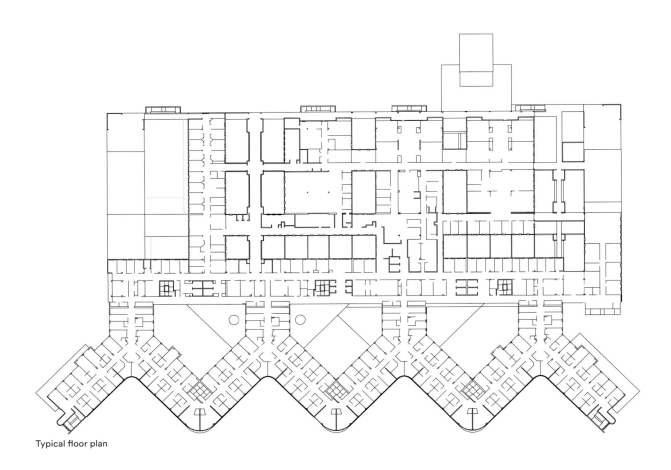

Typical floor plan

Location Lorient, France
Client Centre Hospitalier de Bretagne Sud
Area 700,000 ft² (65,000 m²)
Photography Julien Lanoo, CHBS

Like an ocean swell, the long white façade of the new hospital in Lorient unfolds its undulations to offer patients a panorama of the city center and the Scorff, the river that enters the Atlantic south of Lorient.

The concept entails identifying the major functions as separate volumes (wards, operating units, logistical zones) that are organized for functional proximity. In its work on hospitals, Valode & Pistre have recognized and separated two distinct environments—that of the medico-technical area, a quasi-industrial, high-performance facility able to adapt to all kinds of medical innovations and emergencies, and that of the wards and reception areas, with their comfortable, hotel-like or even domestic feel.

The project not only offers reassurance for the patients and efficiency for the staff, but also maximum modularity and the possibility of extension of independent sectors.

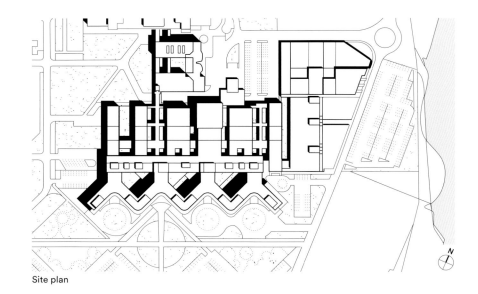

Site plan

2012 Lille Main Stadium

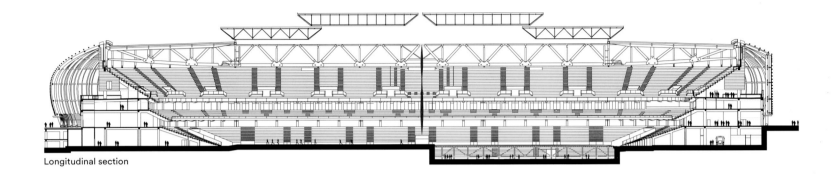
Longitudinal section

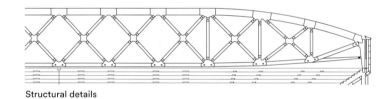
Structural details

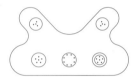

Location Lille, France
Client LMCU (Communauté Urbaine de Lille)
Area 797,000 ft² (74,000 m²)
Photography Max Lerouge, Julien Lanoo

Both a 50,000-seat stadium and a flexible performance venue, the main Stade in Lille has been noted for the originality of its architecture and its mixed-use program.

Enveloped by a translucent shell with rounded angles, the stadium has an immense luminous screen that forms its urban façade. A movable roof consisting of two sliding panels enables the open-air stadium to be converted into an immense covered hall.

Another arena, located under the movable playing field, appears as a prolongation of the stands. This arrangement multiplies the types of sports and performances the new facility can host and allows the facility to be operative much more than the average of twenty-five days a year in most football stadiums.

This project was carried out with Atelier Ferret Architectures as an associate.

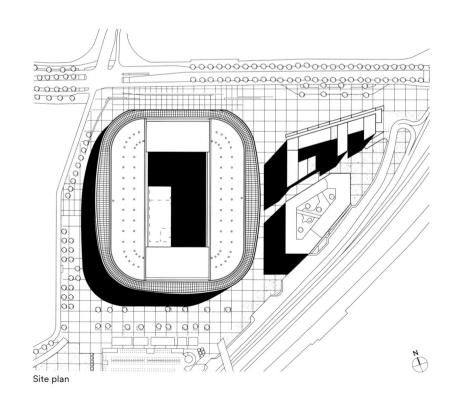
Site plan

2013 Beaugrenelle Paris

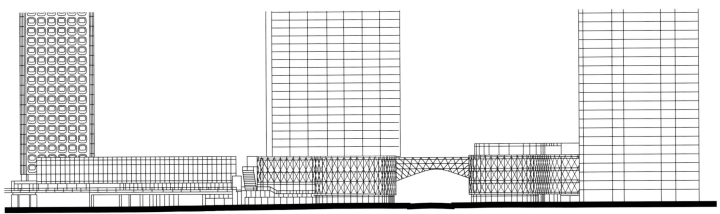
West elevation

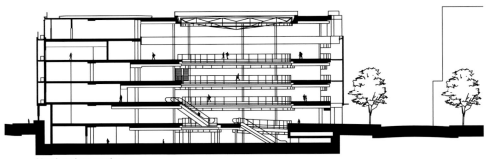
North atrium section

Location Paris, France
Client Apsys / Gecina
Area 807,000 ft² (75,000 m²)
Certification HQE, BREEAM 'Very Good'
Photography Martin Argyroglo, Philippe Chancel

The restructuring and extension of the Beaugrenelle shopping center make it representative of a new generation of urban shopping and leisure centers. Located in the Front de Seine district, a legacy of the utopian urban development of the 1960s, the new Beaugrenelle was an opportunity to redefine urban living and to give shopping a new place in the city. Silk-screened glazing, the only material used for the façade, along with the fluidity and simplicity of the volumes give the complex a very strong identity. Beyond the shops located at street level, the shopping spaces are accessed by two atriums located in the middle of each of the city blocks that make up the center.

On either side of the Pont de Grenelle, the corners of the two blocks define an entry gate into the 15th arrondissement of Paris. With its architecture, Beaugrenelle seeks to appeal to the senses of its visitors, in short, to provide the pleasure of physically experiencing an urban location as opposed to the abstraction, and individualism of online shopping.

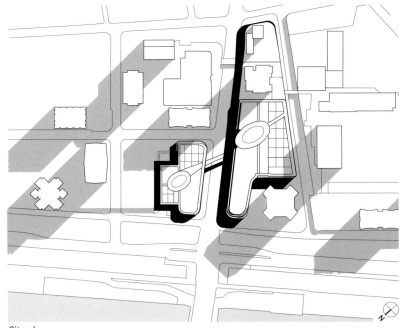
Site plan

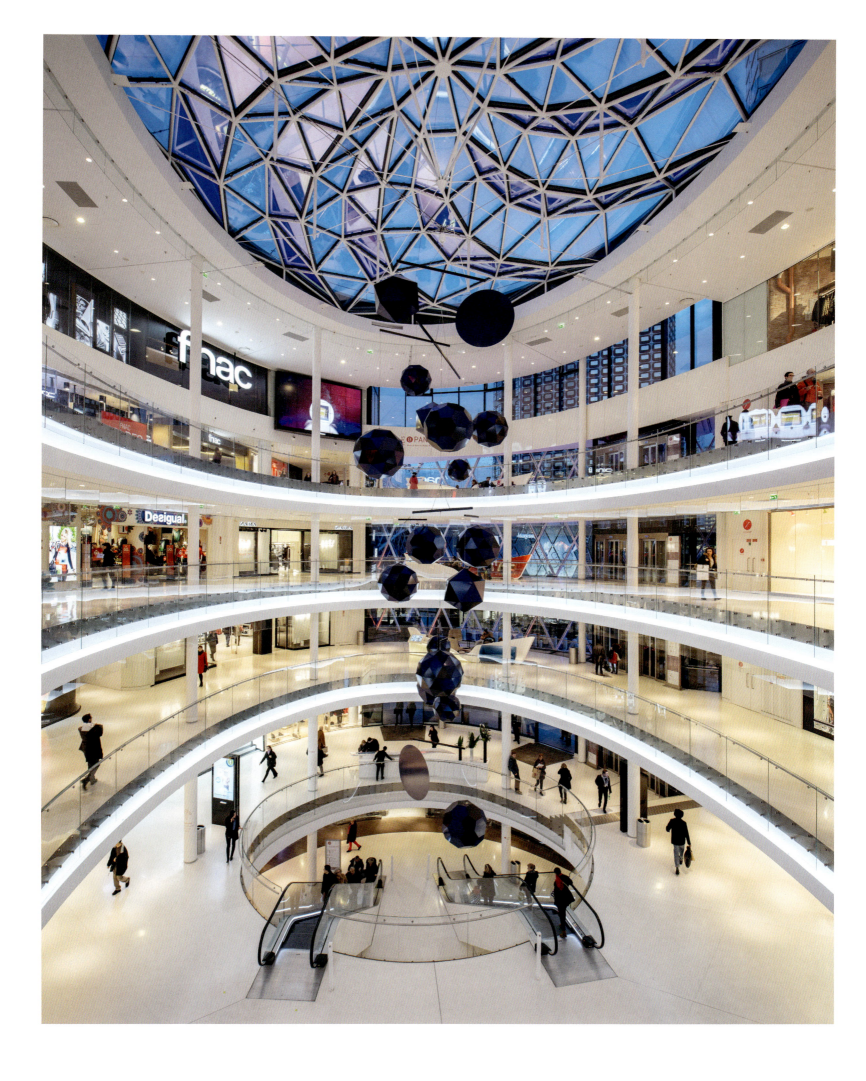

2013 Shenyang Culture Hub

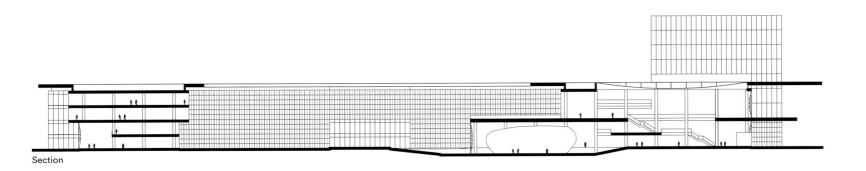
Section

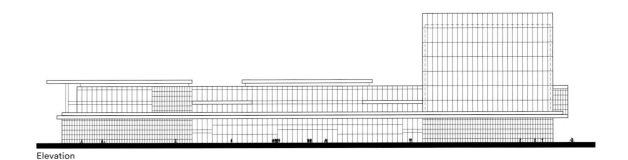
Elevation

Location Shenyang, China
Client Province de Liaoning
Area 4,306,000 ft² (400,000 m²)
Photography Valode & Pistre

Shenyang is the capital of Liaoning province in Manchuria, China. It has a population of over seven million people. It is an ancient city where evidence of farming can be traced back to 5200 BC.

In the framework of the extension scheme for the city, Shenyang decided to create a huge cultural and administrative hub comprising a library, an art museum, a museum of science and technology, and the archives of Liaoning Province. The program covers a total of 4,306,000 square feet (400,000 square meters) on a vast 247-acre (100-hectare) site.

The overall principle involved creating a huge public square flanked on either side by two pairs of aligned, tall buildings. The four buildings have more or less the same floor area—about 1,176,000 square feet (100,000 square meters) on four levels. They have similar massing and an architectural design characterized by large overhanging slabs. In addition to these shared basic characteristics, each building has its own clearly defined architectural identity, arising from its individual program.

The gardens—some planted, some entirely mineral—were designed in accordance with Chinese cultural precepts.

The archive building features a nine-story tower devoted to document conservation. The envelope of the building includes ancient calligraphic elements chosen with representatives of the archives on the basis of historic research.

2013 Shimao Tower

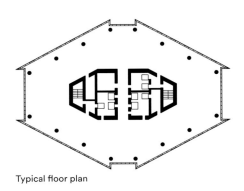

Typical floor plan

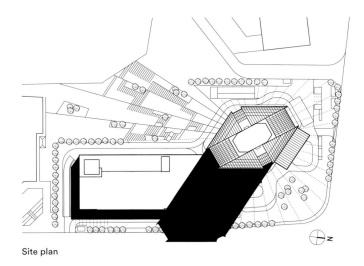

Site plan

Location Fuzhou, China
Client Shimao Group
Area 969,000 ft² (90,000 m²)
Photography Liu Jian

This tower is the flagship component of a large construction project organized around a large park featuring a lake. The tallest building in the city of Fuzhou in eastern China, it marks the skyline with its height and silhouette.

Taking root in a vast garden, the tower rises like a bamboo stalk and blossoms like a lotus flower.

Comprising offices, residential units, and a five-star hotel, the tower's mixed-use program is complemented by shopping facilities. The floor plates, set in an efficient diamond pattern, enjoy a panoramic view of the city and its environs.

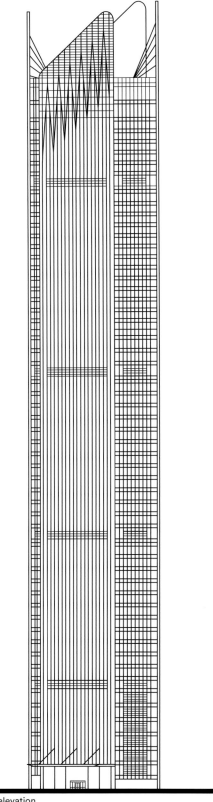

East elevation

2013 L'Ilo

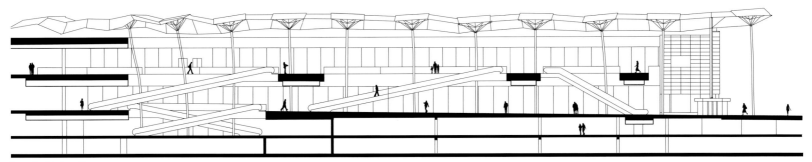
Longitudinal section

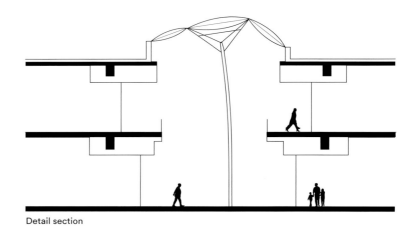
Detail section

Location Epinay-sur-Seine, France
Client Auchan / Immochan
Area 388,000 ft² (36,000 m²)
Certification BREEAM 'Excellent,' HQE
Photography Philippe Chancell

Today in a state of urban decay, the town center of Epinay-sur-Seine, located 6.8 miles (11 kilometers) north of Paris, is the target of a profound urban renovation program.

The reconstruction of the existing shopping center is an opportunity to make it the primary retail heart of the city. The new project segments the shopping center into three clearly defined city blocks and creates two open streets that intersect at a central square. The streets are covered and shaded by a forest of allegorical trees with metal trunks and branches supporting a green canopy to which the use of ETFE (ethylene tetra fluorine ethylene) confers lightness and durability.

The trees emerging from the 388,000-square-foot (36,000-square-meter) site are the shopping center's emblem and illustrate the project's environmental ambitions.

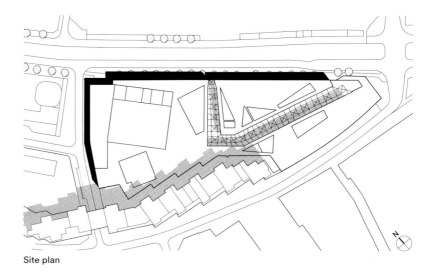
Site plan

2014 Promenade Sainte-Catherine

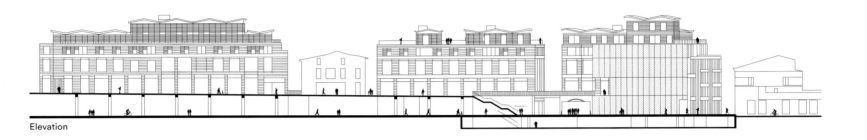

Elevation

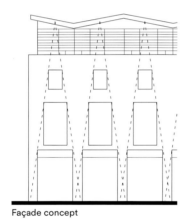

Façade concept

Location Bordeaux, France
Client Redevco
Area 296,000 ft² (27,500 m²)
Photography Valode & Pistre, Jean-François Tremege

The shopping and residential area of Place Sainte-Catherine is becoming a favored new destination in Bordeaux.

Pedestrians discover the district, located in the heart of the historic city, as they walk along newly laid shopping streets. The path of these streets leads to a new square built around a basin, an evocation of the ancient port.

A memorable element, an expressively sculptural building called the Totem is the emblem of the square. The resolutely contemporary architecture is integrated into the traditional historical fabric by using local materials, such as Bordeaux stone, light-colored brick, rubble stone, wood, and terra cotta. The façades are both ordered and varied, and are embellished by works of art.

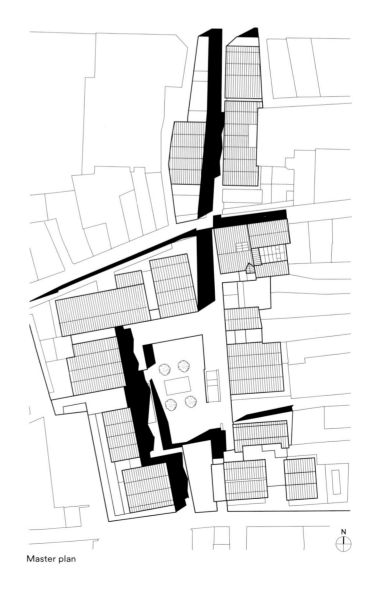

Master plan

2014 Clarins Headquarters

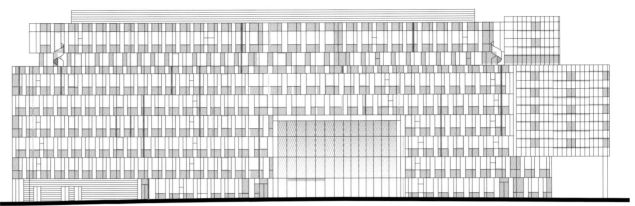
South elevation

Location Neuilly sur Seine, France
Client Bouygues Immobilier
Area 215,000 ft² (20,000 m²)
Certification HQE, BREEAM, and BBC
Photography Julien Lanoo, Augusto da Silva

Located between Paris and the more suburban area of Neuilly near the Porte Maillot, this building seeks to fulfill urban, environmental, and societal goals for the luxury cosmetics group Clarins.

A four-story central hall and garden makes use of glass rectangles with a silk screening that becomes denser as it rises to reduce solar gain. The façade alternates glazing with red vertical bands, gold coloring, and opaque white surfaces, a bit like a textured cloth.

The building was conceived something like a house, with an entrance, garden, and central stairway that unites the seven levels and dining room where a very large table expresses the idea of conviviality.

Office space occupies the better part of the building, with natural light, views to the outside, and a careful choice of materials creating ideal working conditions. The entire project was conceived with a concern for the environment, using the strictest standards of insulation, and other elements such as rooftop solar panels. The natural air ventilation of the entrance hall was inspired by the design of termite nests.

"Termite nests in warm countries have a very sophisticated design that permits the regulation of temperatures through a system of chimneys," explains Denis Valode.

"This is the idea we used in the building. The air in the garden is taken from a 46-foot-deep (14-meter-deep) well where there is a steady temperature and then brought through a horizontal system that runs beneath the foundations of the building. It then goes up and out in part through the sculptural, colored wall in the entrance hall."

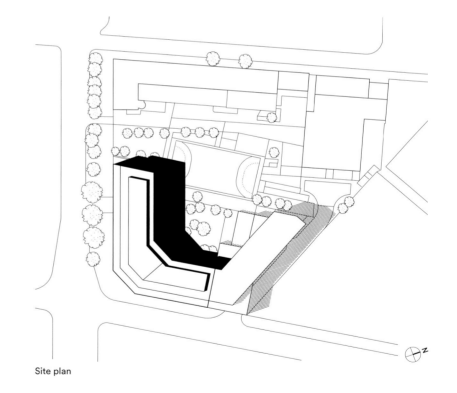
Site plan

2015 Beirut Souks

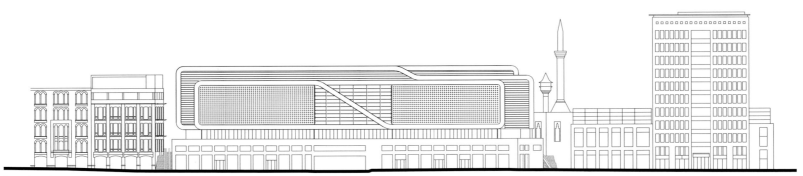

East elevation

Location Beirut, Lebanon
Client Solidere
Date 2015
Area 301,000 ft² (28,000 m²)
Photography Julien Lanoo

A by-product of the international competition for the renovation of the souks (covered markets) in Beirut, of which Valode & Pistre were winners, this leisure activities center includes a cinema complex, restaurants, and shops.

It is set in the continuity of the restored façades typical of the French quarter of Beirut and engages in dialogue with the commercial part of the souks, as designed by Rafael Moneo. The center is intended as an urban project playing a role in the spatial definition of the squares and streets.

Its sculptural morphology, made up of an assembly of metal ribbons forming a coppery arabesque in space, and its façades, animated with points of light that form changing images, make the 301,000-square-foot (28,000-square-meter) building an emblem of the new, nocturnal life of Beirut.

Valode & Pistre worked with the associated architect AKK on this project.

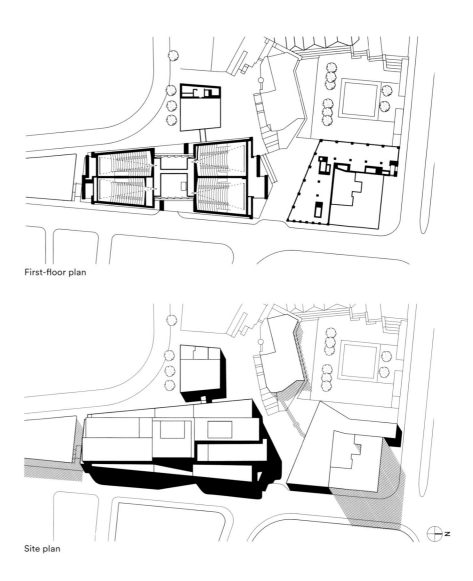

First-floor plan

Site plan

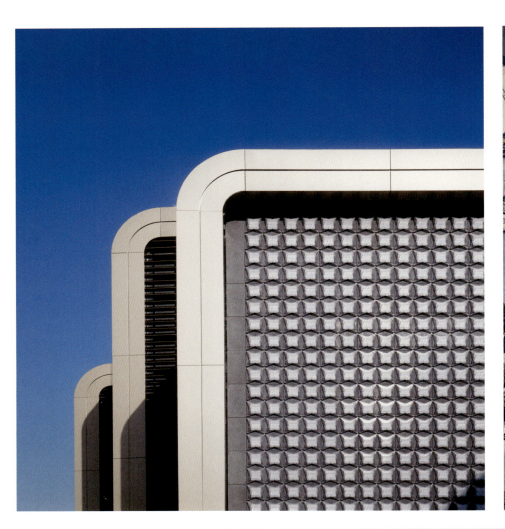

2015 Campus Sanofi

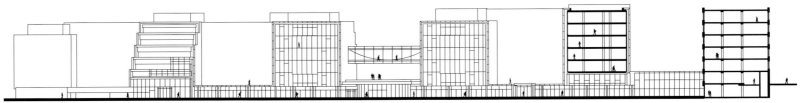
Section

Location Gentilly, France
Client Bouygues Immobilier
Area 549,000 ft² (51,000 m²)
Certification HQE, BREEAM, and BBC
Photography Alexis Paoli

Conceived as an urban campus in Gentilly, which is just 2.5 miles (4 kilometers) south of Paris, the 549,000-square-foot (51,000-square-meter) Val de Bièvre project is a collection of human-scaled buildings that are hinged together and immersed within a lush garden.

The spatial organization of the campus combines functional efficiency and continuity of workspaces within a pleasant and comfortable environment. Interconnected by glazed bridges and covered walkways, the campus buildings are united around a large, landscaped campus commons. The interwoven circulation spaces serve as informal meeting and socializing zones for the campus population.

The promenade, flared to the south, gives the project its identity and defines a landscape opening to the city and the sky. The optimized orientation of the buildings in relation to the path of the sun and the use of high-performance façades specifically adapted to each orientation provide for a campus complex that is very respectful of the environment.

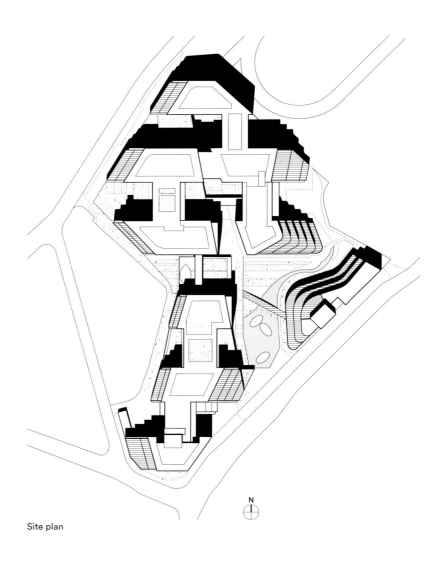
Site plan

2015 Mohammed VI Exhibition Center

South elevation

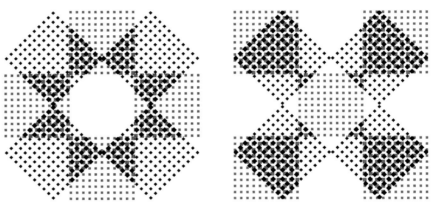

Pattern concept

Location El Jadida, Morocco
Client SOREC Société Royale d'Encouragement du Cheval
Area 1,572,000 ft² (146,000 m²) on a 114-acre (46-ha) site
Photography Valode & Pistre

The Mohammed VI Exhibition Center at El Jadida is a facility with international ambitions whose main activities will focus on Moroccan equestrianism, one of the nation's most popular pursuits.

The exhibition halls are arranged in a coherent, linear fashion, marking out large logistical areas with visitor circulation areas between them. Each hall comprises an open space that is 279 feet (85 meters) wide with neither posts nor columns, and is defined as an independent module from operational, technical, and safety-related points of view.

The main public area, in addition to the esplanade at the entrance, is a linear forecourt linking the halls. This feature, like the local souks (covered markets), is shaded from the sun by a 'pergola,' the construction of which is the result of experimental research carried out with the engineer Nicholas Green.

The long outer wall—the design of which references the architecture of the walled citadel or Kasbah, that of the *mashrabiya* (latticework window), or that of the geometric patterns found on Moroccan Zellige tiles—affirms the identity of the site as soon as visitors arrive.

The project forges its unique identity by drawing its aspirations not only from functional and ergonomic design principles, but also from local climate and culture.

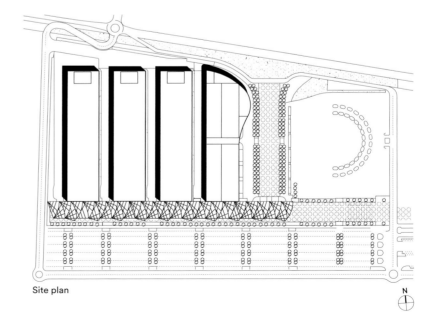

Site plan

2015 Laennec Rive Gauche

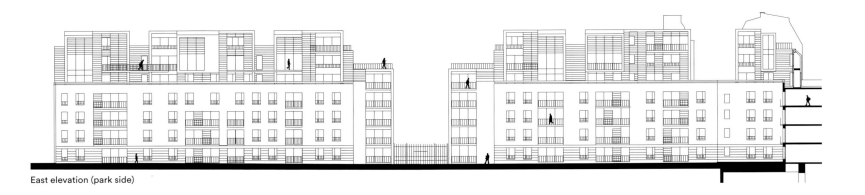

East elevation (park side)

West elevation (street side)

Location Paris, France
Client Cogedim
Area 377,000 ft² (35,000 m²)
Photography Alexis Paoli

Located on the grounds of one of the great historic hospitals of Paris, founded in the seventeenth century, the Laennec project involved the conservation of elements of the old hospital, located in the central 7th arrondissement of Paris.

Façades for the new apartment complex were specifically designed to be integrated into the adjacent streets, the rue Vaneau and the rue de Sèvres. The project is characterized by the reconstruction of a large garden situated in front of the hospital church and in continuity with the nearby gardens. Laennec Rive Gauche includes residential units, a day-care center, and a home for the elderly.

The new residential buildings are aligned along a rectangular plan oriented along the axes of the old hospital, forming a fitting backdrop for the historic buildings.

Comprising a main, continuous volume with discontinuous structures above—like houses placed on the rooftops—the buildings associate contemporary architecture and integration into historical Paris.

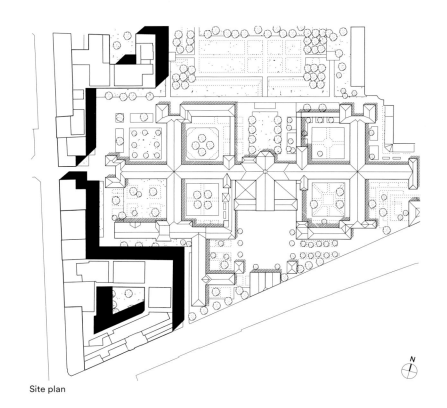

Site plan

2016   Incity Tower

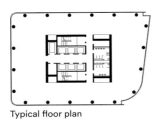
Typical floor plan

Location Lyon, France
Client Sogelym Dixence
Area 431,000 ft² (40,000 m²)
Certification HQE, BREEAM, and BBC
Photography Julien Lanoo

The city of Lyon is not known for its high-rise buildings. Aside from the Tour Part Dieu (541 feet [165 meters]) built in 1975, and despite some pending plans, the newest and tallest tower in the Part Dieu district, Incity, is nestled within the existing urban grid of Lyon, providing a dynamic addition to the skyline of the city.

Aligned with the corner of the rue Garibaldi and the Cours Lafayette, and with welcoming expanses of glass open to passers-by, this state-of-the-art tower participates actively in the organization and restructuring of the evolving Part Dieu district of Lyon.

Its slender peak tops out at 656 feet (200 meters) and provides an elegant visual apex to the composition of existing towers due to rise up around the project site. Aligned north–south along the axis of the Rhône and Saône rivers, the tower is oriented in the direction of the prevailing winds.

The façades exposed to the sun are draped in a protective veil, reminiscent of a cocoon—an important symbol, related to the silk weaving history of Lyon. This envelope consists of a ventilated double-glazed façade that provides for the comfort and convenience of the tower users and improves the tower's energy performance.

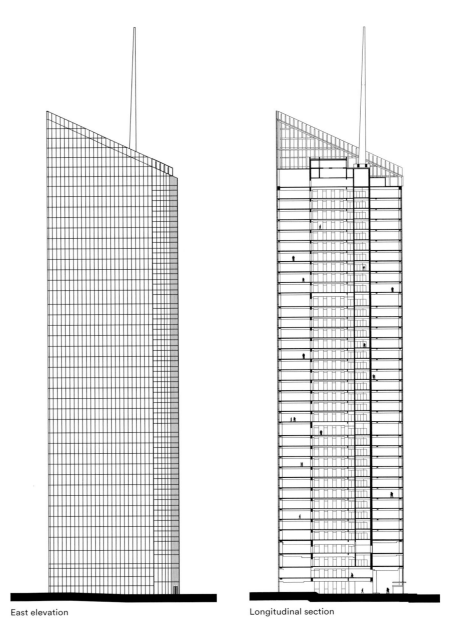
East elevation   Longitudinal section

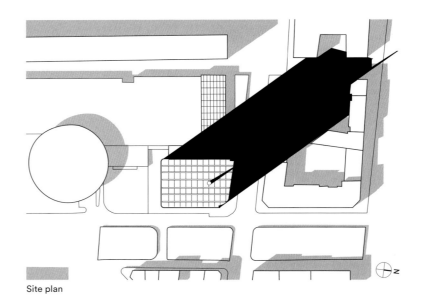
Site plan

170

2016 Airbus Group Leadership University

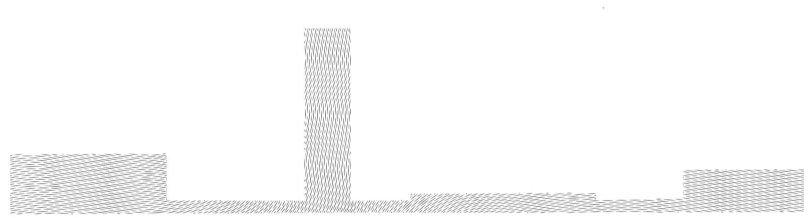

Façade concept

Location Toulouse, France
Client Immobilière AELIS / Airbus
Area 138,000 ft² (12 800 m²) on a 10-acre (4-ha) site
Photography Philippe Chancel

The Airbus Group University Campus project is designed to bring together the group's top managers for training. It features a hotel, a restaurant, a training center, and a convention and events center.

The complex is located at the airport hub in Toulouse. The challenge was to create a complex on the scale of the site, and, above all, to express the cultural identity of this international group via a functional and memorable architectural design.

The different functional sections of the project are symbolically brought together in a large circle of 262 feet (80 meters) in diameter, surrounded by a circular gallery. The cylinder that makes up the curved façade consists of large coiled white slats forming a sculptural structure suggesting the airflow along an aircraft wing. This façade has a lighting system designed by Yann Kersalé.

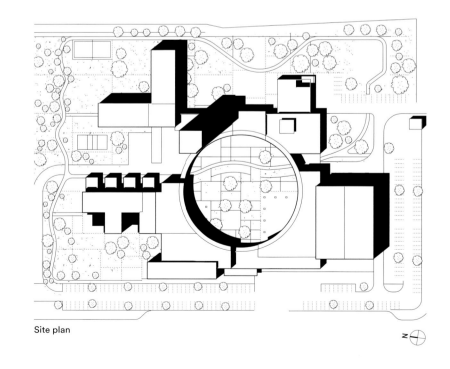

Site plan

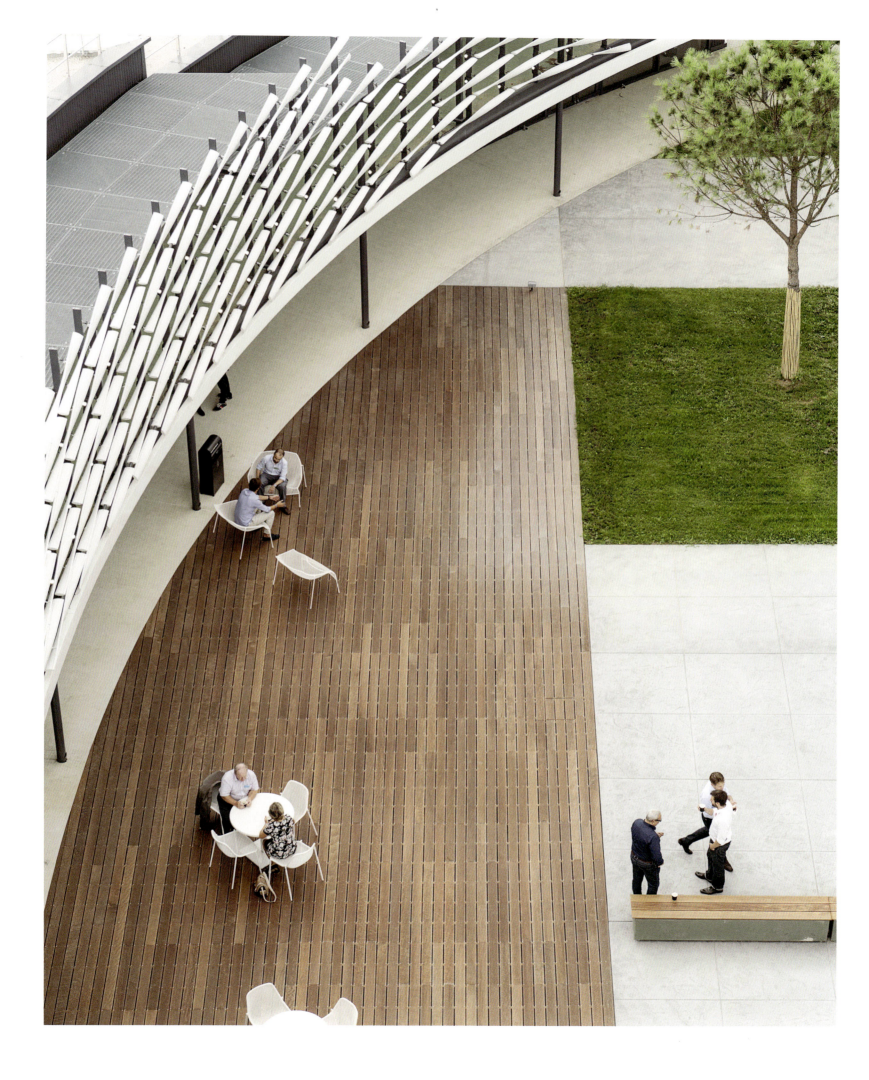

2016 Damac Tower

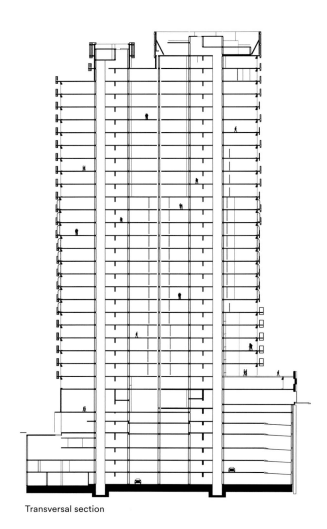

Transversal section

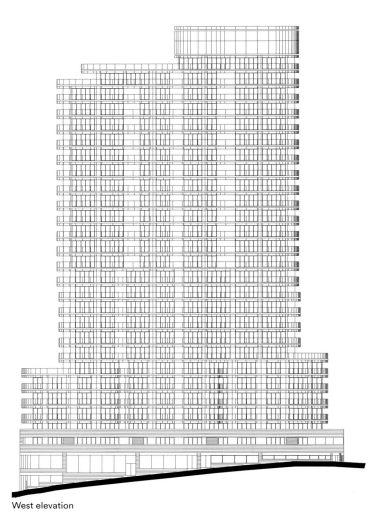

West elevation

Location Beirut, Lebanon
Client Damac Properties
Area 323,000 ft² (30,000 m²)
Photography Bernard Khalil

Winner of a competition organized by Damac Properties, this planned project for a residential tower (La Résidence Tower) is located in the Marine Area of Beirut, on the seafront. Framed by other towers, it stands out from its neighbors with a silhouette made up of a superposition of undulating volumes that responds to the perpetual motion of the sea.

Contrasted with the rigor of the floor plan of the apartments—organized on an orthogonal grid—the envelope is free and is deformed on each level to profit off the panoramic views of the Mediterranean as much as possible.

The tower accommodates simple, duplex, and triplex apartments, as well as a swimming pool in its highest part.

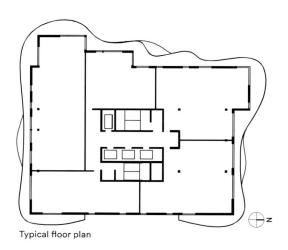

Typical floor plan

2016   BioMérieux Headquarters

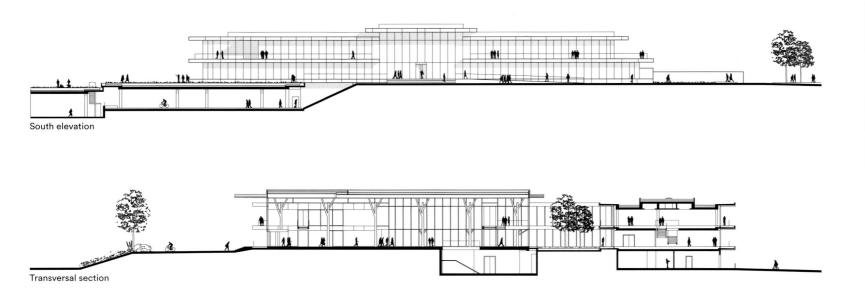

South elevation

Transversal section

Location Marcy-l'Etoile, France
Client Sogelym Dixence
Area 108,000 ft² (10,000 m²)
Photography Philippe Chancel

This is a headquarters for an international biotechnology company, located in Marcy-l'Etoile near Lyon.

As is frequently the case in their corporate structures, the architects decided to create a large, covered atrium, bordered by the corporate restaurant. The two-story structure has a square plan and is characterized by light-gray prefabricated concrete slabs that project out, at the first floor and the top of the building, providing sun shading.

Bands of full-height glazing at the ground and first levels give an impression of lightness and also allow daylight to enter the building without excessive solar gain. On the upper level, the design allows for the creation of either open or partitioned offices, with the possibility to change the configurations at will.

Several characteristics of the work of Valode & Pistre are in evidence here. Starting with a simple, strong modern appearance they succeed in creating convivial meeting places, such as the atrium, while offering a maximum degree of flexibility in office arrangements. At odds with architects who seek to shock or to render their work identifiable for formal reasons, Valode & Pistre seek modernity in its clearest and most efficient forms.

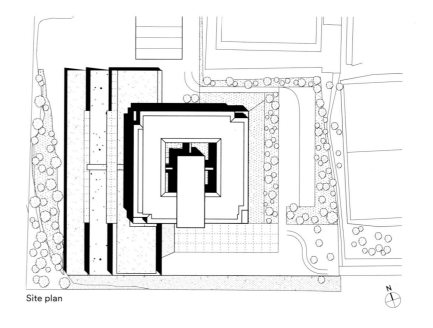

Site plan

2016 Gonesse Hospital

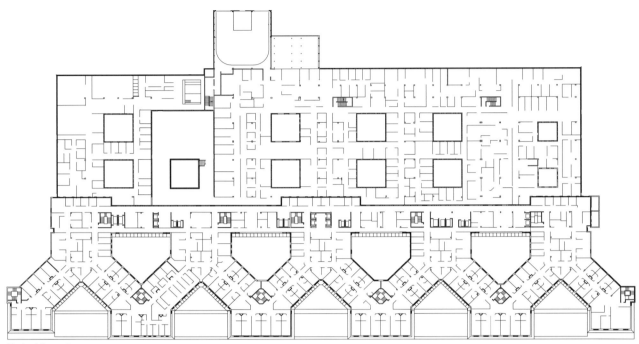

Typical floor plan

Location Gonesse, France
Client Centre Hospitalier de Gonesse
Area 861,000 ft² (80,000 m²)
Photography Philippe Chancel

The new MCO (medical, surgical, obstetrics) building, the key element in the restructuring of the 61.7-acre (25-hectare) Gonesse hospital campus in the northeastern suburbs of Paris, is designed like a residential building set in a park.

Its functional principle lies in a distinction between consultation and patient housing, 70 percent of which has panoramic views facing the park, while the medico-technical areas face towards the rear.

Precisely conceived, the technical block is clad in metal—neat and clean like the blouse of the clinician. A central axis gathers all traffic and links the two zones.

The architecture stands out opposite the park because of its form, which resembles pavilions that marry white polished concrete and wood-toned blinds in a strict, measured design that evokes Japanese palaces, with their serenity and relation to nature. The added elements of the complex have an area of 861,000 square feet (80,000 square meters).

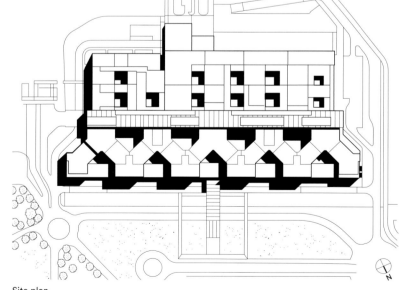

Site plan

2017 University of Toulouse—Jean Jaurès

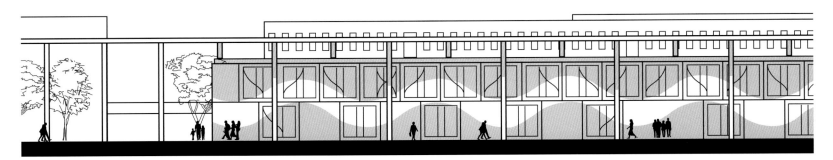

Façade detail

Elevation

Location Toulouse, France
Client Miralis (Vinci)
Area 646,000 ft² (60,000 m²)
Photography Philippe Chancel

The reconstruction in the heart of Toulouse of Mirail University, now re-baptized Jean Jaurès University, is the latest stage in a wide-ranging program designed to bring the institution into the fold of major European universities.

The architecture of the university, developed with the French philosopher Michel Serres, is a three-dimensional network of connections between teaching staff, students, and researchers, and between knowledge production, dissemination, and sharing. The Greek-French architect Georges Candilis (1913–1995), the designer of the first buildings on the site, here inspires the scheme designed to knit together the entire Mirail site. The work with Michel Serres focused on the meaning of the university as a location when faced with the dematerialization of educational communication.

Team-sport facilities have been placed at the heart of the project, while a street/atrium crosses the university, lined with a range of social facilities, forming a link between the city's northern and southern districts.

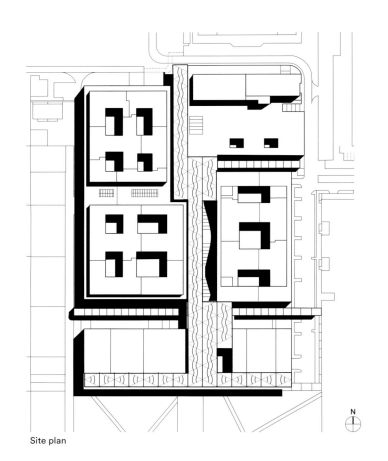

Site plan

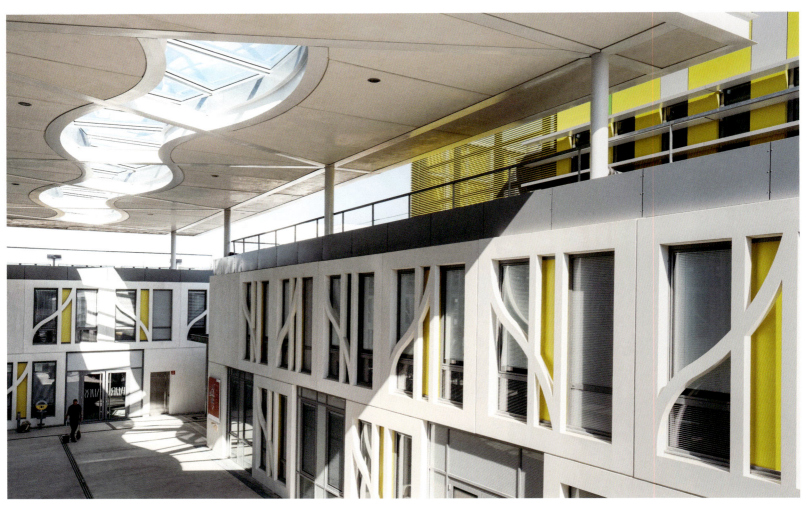

2017 Regional Judiciary Police Department

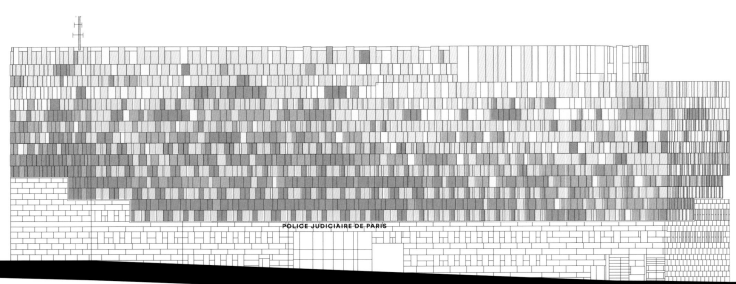

East elevation

Location Paris, France
Client Ministère de l'Intérieur
Area 350,000 ft² (32,500 m²)
Photography Philippe Chancel

The Regional Judiciary Police Department in the Batignolles neighborhood of Paris near the Porte de Clichy comprises a striking sculpted urban structure with a floor area of 350,000 square feet (32,500 square meters).

By turns solid and ephemeral, the building stands out with its contrasting features that reflect and reinforce its surroundings, particularly the ancient Thiers Wall (1841–44) and the new Judiciary City of Paris complex designed by Renzo Piano.

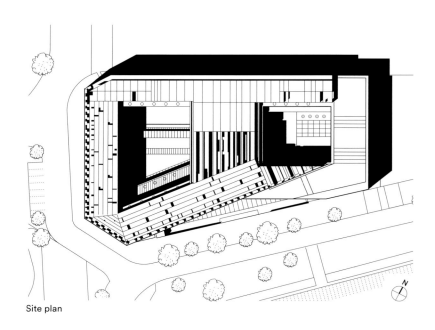

Site plan

2017 Paris Convention Centre, Pavilion 7

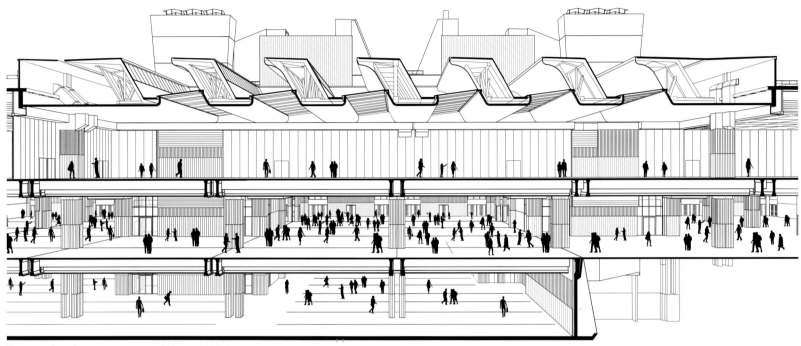

Transversal section

Location Paris, France
Client Viparis
Area 807,000 ft² (75,000 m²)
Photography Philippe Chancel

The renovation project for Pavilion 7 formed part of a wide-ranging renovation and modernization scheme for the Parc des Expositions at Porte de Versailles in Paris.

Pavilion 7 is the most important part of this operation, in which Valode & Pistre had been involved since 1995, and its completion forms a significant addition to the transformation of Paris Expo Porte de Versailles.

Characteristic of the 'brutalist' movement of the 1960s and 1970s, the impressive raw concrete megastructure (65.6 × 65.6 feet [20 × 20 meters] on three levels), enclosed in concrete panels, was stripped of its secondary elements so that it appears in all its power. This made it possible to fit the building with modern exhibition facilities of the highest standards and to create a convention center with a capacity of 15,000 people.

Once opaque, the building is now transparent. An entirely glazed façade offers views of Paris and the Eiffel Tower.

Site plan

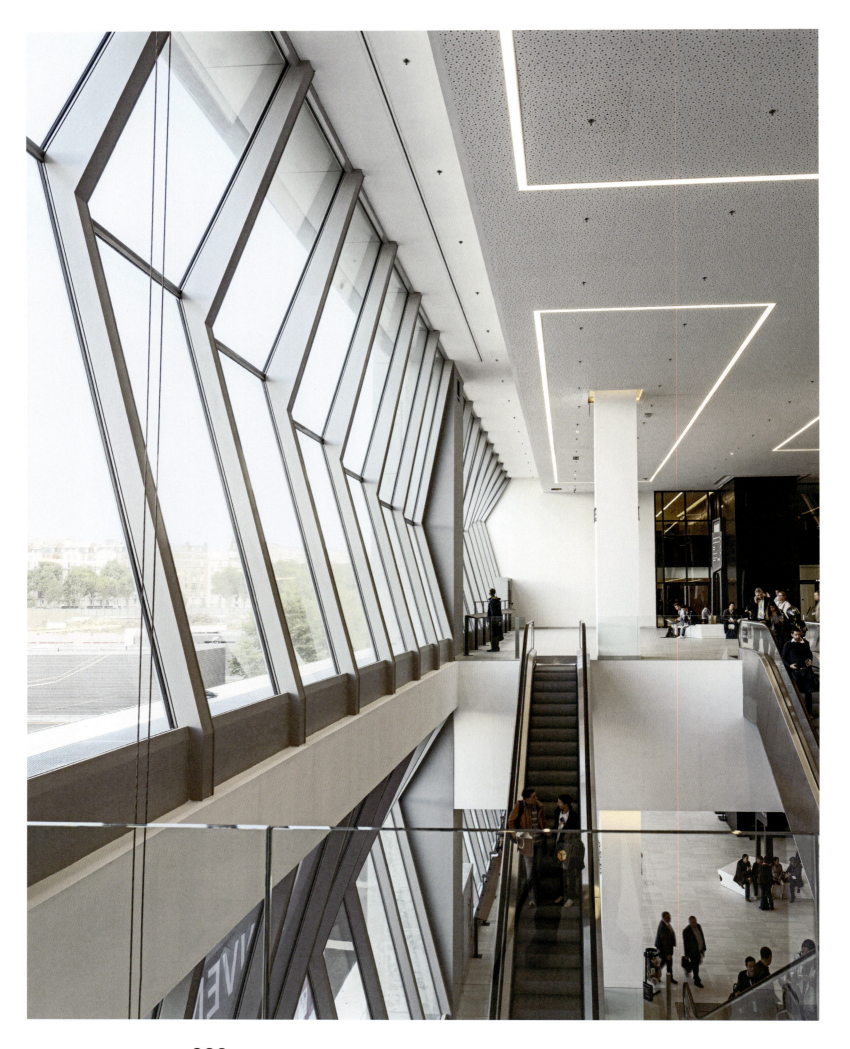

2017 Shenzhen Hospital

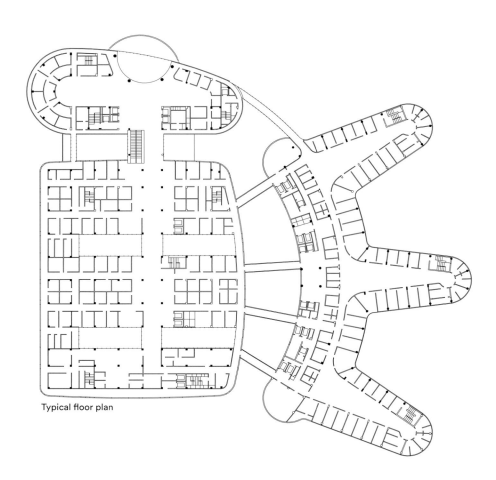
Typical floor plan

Location Shenzhen, China
Client Pingshan New District Development and Finance Administration
Area 1,044,000 ft² (97,000 m²)
Photography Valode & Pistre

The hospital design includes a six-story outpatient and emergency building, a five-story medical and technological management building, an eight-story inpatient building, and supporting areas.

Although the facilities are independent, they are also closely connected and, as per their hospital projects, the architects sought to create sufficient structural flexibility to accommodate future developments in healthcare. The movement of staff, patients, and visitors is carefully planned for maximum efficiency and minimum interference. The hospital's capacity is 600 beds, and the project also includes 469 underground parking spots and 131 further spaces at ground level.

As the architects observed that the cell is the basic structural unit of all living organisms, so too the building is the fundamental unit in human life and activity. Great attention was paid to the use of energy-saving, environmentally friendly technology to reduce carbon emissions and to create an ecological hospital.

Glass walls, where possible, connect the inside with the surrounding greenery. A rooftop garden is also part of the design. The low-e glass curtain walls are shielded from the sun by external shutters in wood or terra cotta. Courtyards were scattered around the medical and technological building, inpatient ward areas, and outpatient building. Metal sheeting was employed in the elevation of the medical and technological building.

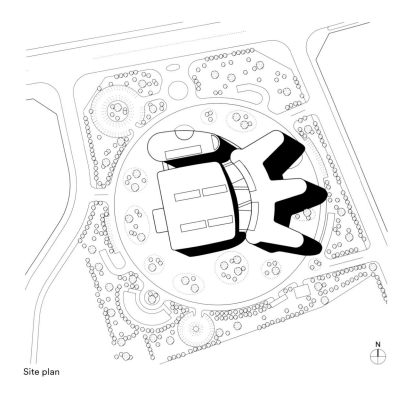
Site plan

204

2018 Skolkovo Innovation Center

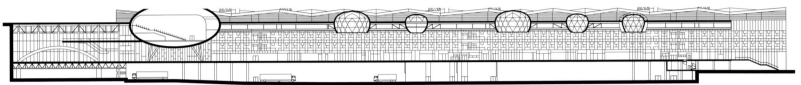
Longitudinal section

Location Moscow, Russia
Client Skolkovo Innovation Center
Area 1,292,000 ft² (120,000 m²)
Photography Alexeï Naroditsky

Skolkovo, not far from the heart of Moscow, embodies the Russian ambition to develop medical, economic, nuclear, space, and biological research, fostering new discoveries and developing them commercially. More of a town than a campus, the 988-acre (400-hectare) site will include, in addition to research establishments, homes for 3000 people, hotels, a convention center, a university, a start-up complex, a Technopark, and cultural facilities.

Working with the Urban Council Presidency, Valode & Pistre were given the task of coordinating this large project, which involves other architects, such as Herzog & de Meuron. Valode & Pistre were also entrusted with the detailed design of a Technopark, laboratories for firms developing cutting-edge technologies, housing, and several other facilities. The master plan for the district is a contemporary interpretation of the villages of the Russian plains.

With a floor area of 2,153,000 square feet (200,000 square meters), the Technopark brings together leading-edge laboratories and the flexible, reconfigurable reception areas for the start-ups. It is, above all, a forum for multidisciplinary interaction and exchange designed to foster the development of innovations.

With its huge atrium, skylight domes, broad walkways overlooking a garden where a futuristic auditorium is located, and a long black façade stretching 984 feet (300 meters) into the forest, the architecture of the Technopark offers a synthesis of Russian scientific creativity and rigorous experimental and inventive processes.

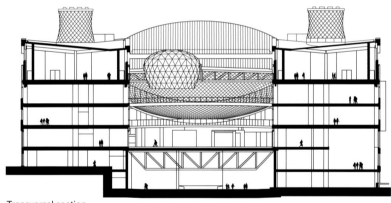
Transversal section

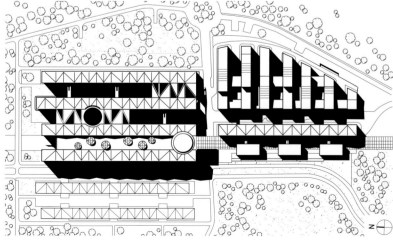
Site plan

2019 Shenzhen Exhibition Center

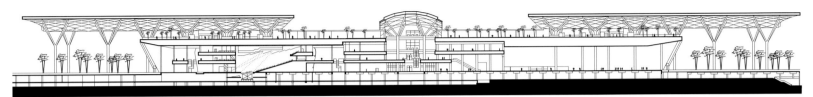

Transversal section

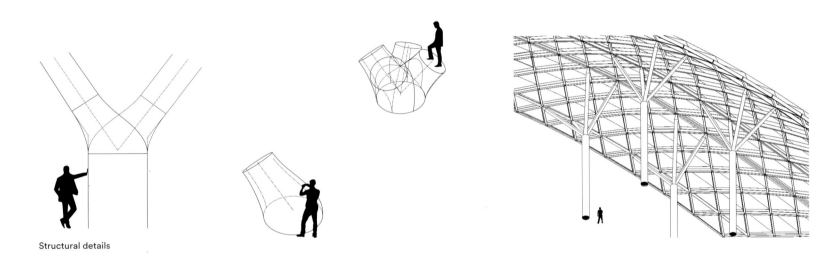

Structural details

Location Shenzhen, China
Client Shenzhen Investments Holding Co.
Area 9,150,000 ft² (850,000 m²)
Photography Philippe Chancel

Valode & Pistre won an international competition to design the New Shenzhen International Convention & Exhibition Center (SZICEC).

Located near Shenzhen Bao'an International Airport, the complex will have a floor area of 9,150,000 square feet (850,000 square meters), making it the largest exhibition center in the world. The architects insist not only on the exceptional size of this complex but also on the fact that its appearance from approaching aircraft is an essential element in the design.

The scale of this project is indeed urban, and it is clear that Valode & Pistre not only master the design of exhibition buildings, such as the ones in Paris at the Porte de Versailles, but also that their grasp of contemporary construction technology is such that they were judged by the city to be the most obvious choice for the design given the rapid construction schedule.

There are to be eighteen standard exhibition halls and one double-size unit as well as more than 1,000,000 square feet (93 square meters) of meeting space. Set on a site of nearly 338.5 acres (137 hectares), the facility is to replace the previous SZICEC complex, completed in 2001.

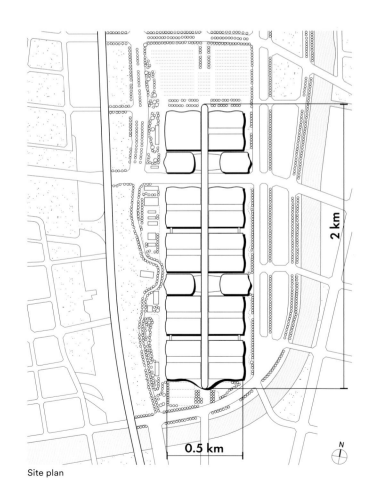

Site plan

2019 Paris Expo, Pavilion 6

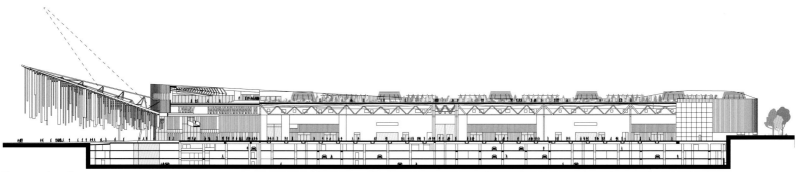

Transversal section

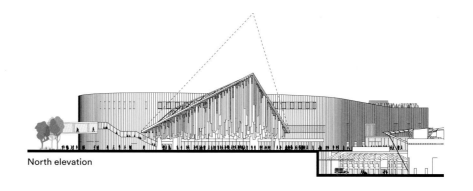

North elevation

Location Paris, France
Client Viparis
Area 2,303,477 ft² (214,000 m²)
Photography Philippe Chancel

The Pavilion 6 project, and the new district it generates, is a key stage in the complete restructuring of the Porte de Versailles Exhibition Center, to ensure both its reinforcement at the international level and its integration in Paris.

It thus becomes the center of a new district organized around two squares.

Pavilion 6 is conceived as a large volume with rounded and fluid forms, whose internal constitution manages the great complexity of the site in a simple and obvious way: its multidirectional geometry; its considerable differences in levels—32.8 feet (10 meters); its intertwined zones, circuits, and logistical access; its three-level parking base; and its connections and visitor paths.

On the roof of Pavilion 6, the event space and the restaurant offer a moment of architecture 'in parentheses'— greenhouses built around an intimate patio-terrace, with a perspective on the plantings activities of the urban farm, Paris, and the sky beyond. A sort of urban and rural refuge, which can be discovered at the top of the monumental staircase.

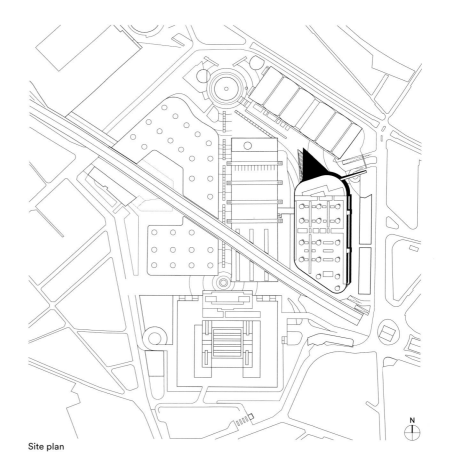

Site plan

2020 Saint-Gobain Tower

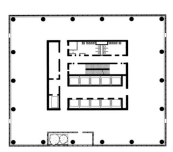

Typical floor plan

Location La Défense, France
Client Generali
Area 538,200 ft² (50,000 m²)
Certification HQE Sustainable Building, LEED Platinum, BREEAM 'Outstanding'
Photography Laurent Kronental, Sergio Grazia

The new Saint-Gobain headquarters is a 558-foot-tall (170-meter-tall) tower with approximately 538,200 square feet (50,000 square meters) of floor space, located in the heart of the La Défense district near Paris.

The architectural and technical aim of this project was to demonstrate that systematically seeking to provide high-quality working conditions and looking for the most effective solutions in environmental and energy terms can combine to form the basis for a new generation of towers. The aim was also to make the tower into a showcase for the expertise and international image of Saint-Gobain, the world's leading manufacturer of high-performance glass materials.

The architectural design of the Saint-Gobain Tower involved playing with light. It consists of a set of 'crystals,' the sides and angles of which, combined with the characteristics of the glass itself, are alternately transparent and reflective.

In terms of massing, the building has three main sections: a main 'trunk' containing most of the offices, and two transparent glass rhombohedrons. The one at the foot of the building houses the public showroom, an auditorium, and restaurant areas under the trees. The one at the top, which is larger, houses Saint-Gobain's public relations and hospitality department, set amid terraced gardens.

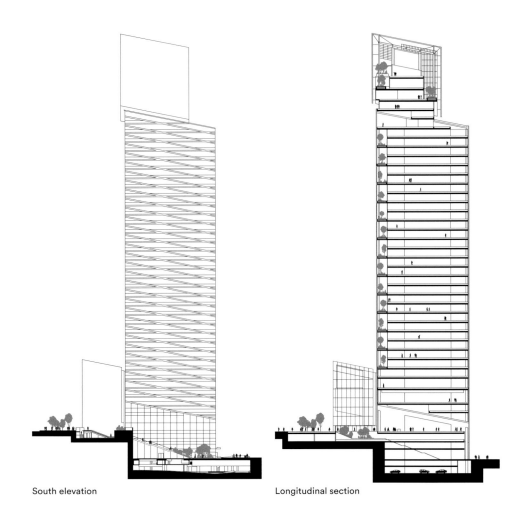

South elevation

Longitudinal section

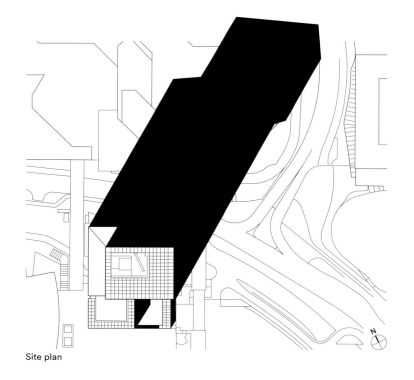

Site plan

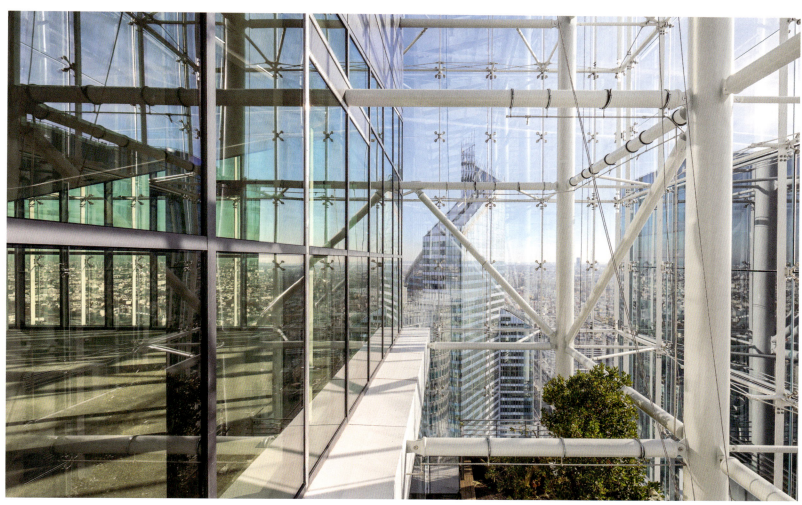

2020   ABC (Autonomous Building for Citizens)

West elevation

Location Grenoble, France
Client Bouygues Immobilier
Area 75,347 ft² (7,000 m²)
Photography Philippe Chancel

The ABC (Autonomous Building for Citizens) is the result of a multidisciplinary research project carried out in partnership with Bouygues Construction R&D and the French Alternative Energies and Atomic Energy Commission.

This research project experiments with the idea of self-sufficiency for housing in terms of energy, water, and the systematic management of waste. The ABC seeks to capture sunlight, to collect rainwater, and to draw the energy it requires from the environment.

The aim of ABC is to constitute a dense urban habitat, with a view to limiting urban sprawl. Each architectural or technical solution is, thus, assessed in terms of its value to society: in what way does it provide an opportunity to facilitate appropriation, to make the user more involved in the built environment, to facilitate social interactions, and to adapt to new lifestyles that characterize changing urban society.

The first experimental complex is being developed at the Ecocité de la Presqu'île in Grenoble, in the form of three buildings comprising approximately 100 social and private housing units.

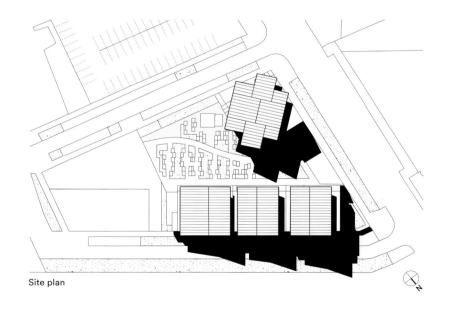

Site plan

2020 Prado Concorde

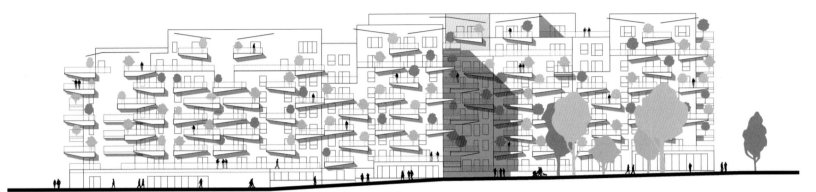

South elevation

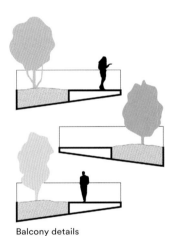

Balcony details

Location Castelnau-le-Lez, France
Client Helenis/Opalia
Area 301,000 ft² (28,000 m²)
Photography Philippe Chancel

Castelnau-le-Lez, a town near Montpellier in the south of France, enjoys a mild Mediterranean climate. The new district of Prado Concorde, on the banks of the River Lez at the entrance to the town, combines residential developments with schools and shops in a large block arranged around a garden in the form of a valley.

The architectural design of the housing units makes maximum use of exterior extensions to allow residents to be outside. An extra exterior 'room' provides each flat with its own additional space, complete with a tree for shade.

To achieve this aim, the project used an innovative concept: a series of large balconies whose triangular shape and variable cross-section make it possible to support their weight on consoles at their thickest point, where the built-in tree containers are. These prefabricated high-performance concrete elements are staggered from one floor to the next to provide the airflow necessary for the trees to grow.

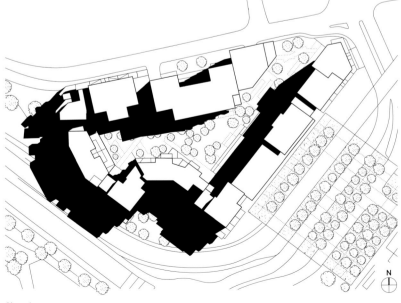

Site plan

2021 Urban Garden

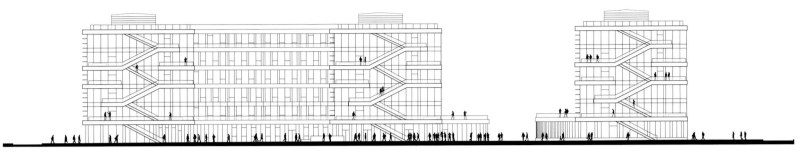

East elevation

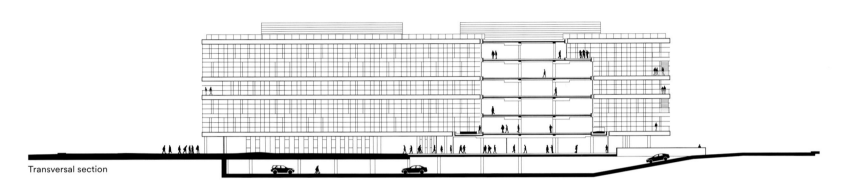

Transversal section

Location Lyon, France
Client Sogelym Dixence
Area 301,000 ft² (28,000 m²)
Photography Philippe Chancel

This tertiary campus project is in the southern part of the 7th arrondissement of Lyon. It consists of three parallel buildings, five stories high and increasing in length from north to south.

The main façades face south and north. The southern façades are protected from solar gain by large continuous sunshades, perfectly effective in this orientation; the north façades are naturally not exposed to the sun in the same way.

The office floors are designed to ensure the greatest possible freedom of layout. The vertical circulation core is reduced to a minimum footprint and the additional stairs, necessary for safety, are set outside the east gable. Combined with external landings, they ensure a complementary relationship between levels. They constitute a repetitive and very significant architectural motif of the project, a symbol of communication. The ground floors are organized according to a flexible and curvilinear design, which seems to develop freely in relation to the rectilinear and parallel bodies of buildings. This fluidity of the ground-floor plan makes it possible to establish a diagonal path and visual permeability through the project and the green spaces between the buildings.

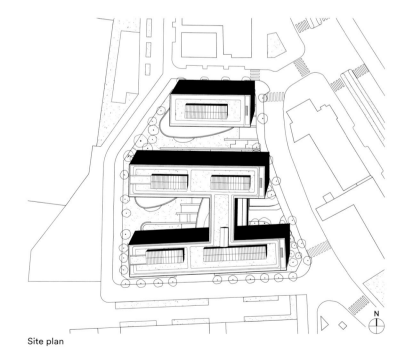

Site plan

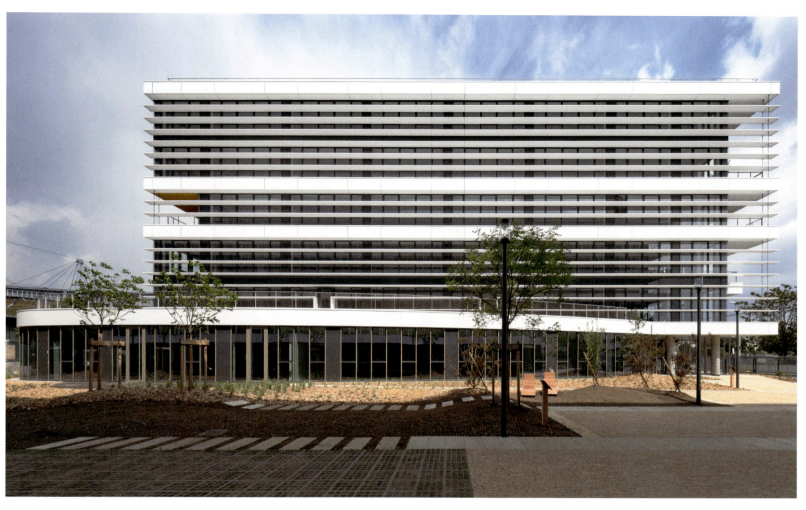

2021 Bulgari Hotel

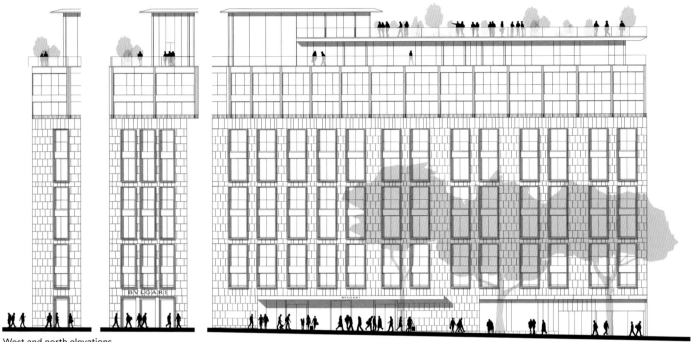

West and north elevations

Location Paris, France
Client SCI 30 AGV
Area 118,403 ft² (11,000 m²)
Photography Philippe Chancel

This 118,403-square-foot (11,000-square-meter) five-star hotel, located at 30 avenue George V (8th arrondissement of Paris), has seventy-five rooms and suites, a restaurant, spa, swimming pool, and panoramic terrace overlooking Paris. Three-quarters of the suites have terraces and loggias, and a penthouse on two floors, benefiting from a 6,458-square-foot (600-square-meter) private garden and a panoramic view on the capital's emblematic monuments.

The architecture of the project, entrusted by Bulgari to Valode & Pistre in association with Antonio Citterio and Patricia Viel, expresses a dialogue between two cultures, Italian and Parisian.

The bay windows of the façades are developed on two levels like Italian palaces, while fitting precisely into the Haussmannian context of Paris.

The interior décor, designed with refinement, combines stones and marbles from different Italian regions with glassworks based on the inherited techniques of René Lalique. The timeless glamor of Bulgari blends with Parisian charm.

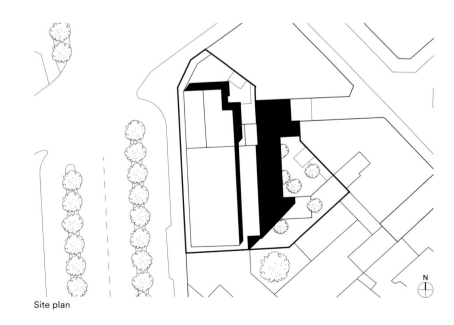

Site plan

2021 Montrouge Academy

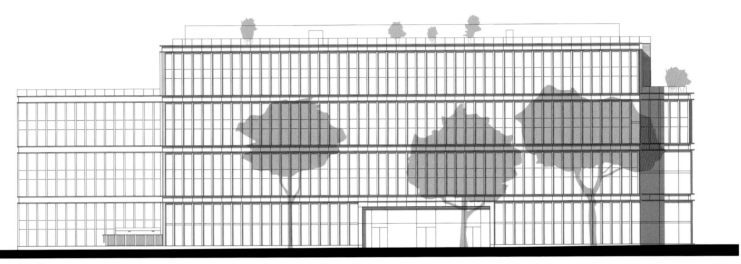

North elevation

Location Montrouge, France
Client SCI 30 AGV
Area *Offices* 355,209 ft² (33,000 m²),
housing 11,840 ft² (1,100 m²)
Photography Philippe Chancel, Kamel Khalfi

The *académie* is a 355,209-square-foot (33,000-square-meter) mixed-use complex of offices and 11,840 square feet (1,100 square meters) of housing located in Montrouge, just to the south of Paris. The project contributes to the architectural and urban improvement of this area.

The proposed plan, simple and efficient, is organized around a vast central patio with trees. The façades, aligned with the streets, are composed according to a double-level play that modifies the perception of the scale of the buildings. The alternating oblique faces of the mullions that punctuate the split floors generate a singular kinetic effect.

A large transparent reception hall, organized on two levels, provides a link between the urban space and the central garden.

The office floors, which also cross between the street and the garden, are naturally and abundantly lit and provide total flexibility in the layout.

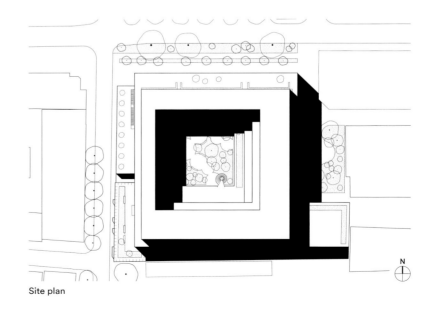

Site plan

2022 Issy—Cœur de Ville

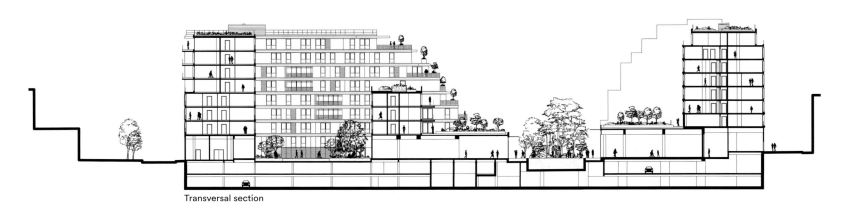
Transversal section

Location Issy-les-Moulineaux, France
Client Altarea-Cogedim
Area 1,184,030 ft² (110,000 m²) on a 7.4-acre (3-ha) site
Photography Valode & Pistre

The concept of this new district, located about 5 miles (7 kilometers) from the center of Paris, is to array buildings around an urban park. This option has a dual purpose, to satisfy the residents' desire for contact with nature but also to be part of the history of the city of Issy-les-Moulineaux. It is a municipality that has developed on the basis of a set of parks formerly belonging to castles or religious communities that have partly disappeared, leaving behind their large green spaces. The park is thus the heart of the new district. The buildings that surround it have been arranged in a stepped pattern to open up the space that is planted beneath the sky, bringing in sunshine. This scheme makes it possible to provide the residences with exterior terraces shaded by pergolas.

This project is also characterized by its functional, generational, and social variety. It combines apartments that are for sale with social housing, organized in five blocks with office buildings divided into three groups. The ground floors are dedicated to shops, restaurants, and brasseries that open onto the central park. There is also a kindergarten, a primary school, accommodations for the elderly, a digital creation workshop, and movie theaters.

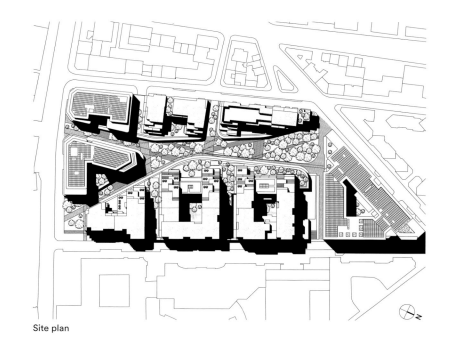
Site plan

2023 Hendrikhof Tilburg

West elevation

Location Tilburg, Netherlands
Client City of Tilburg
Area 365,973 ft² (34,000 m²)
Photography Valode & Pistre

The Hendrikhof project, in the heart of the historic center of Tilburg, reimagines the interior of an urban block, bordering Heuvelstraat, by densifying it and installing houses and shops, thus creating a new entirely pedestrian and eco-friendly neighborhood.

On the theme of the silhouette of aligned gables, typical of Dutch cities, the architecture of the project develops under a large continuous pleat, which varies in height from three floors at the edge of the island to twenty floors at the center, to create a tower, the highest point of the composition, necessary for densification and a new emblem of the city.

This folded line accompanies the layout of the street, conceived as an open-air shopping center, at a friendly and intimate scale inspired by the Place Furstemberg. The historic buildings on the street have been carefully restored, while the architecture inside the block is sober and contemporary, using the light-colored brick, characteristic of Tilburg.

Between modernity and respect for the historical context, boldness of scale, and integration into the low-rise urban fabric, the project aims to add a new dimension and a new attractiveness to the city of Tilburg.

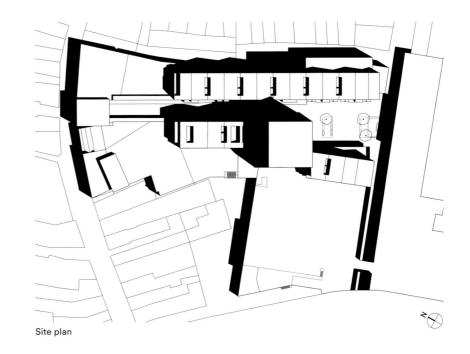

Site plan

2025 Les Ardoines Station
(Grand Paris Express Station)

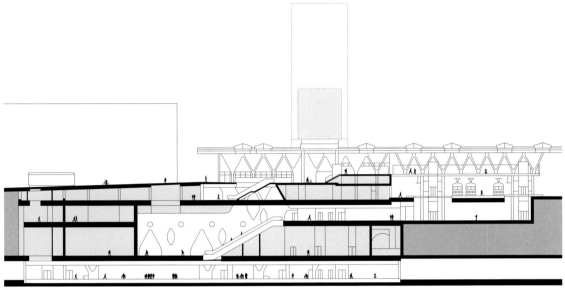
Section

Location Vitry-sur-Seine, France
Client Société du Grand Paris
Area 75,347 ft² (7,000 m²)
Photography Valode & Pistre

This station for the Grand Paris regional express network was designed to be below student and family accommodations that constitute a bridge building and a small tower.

The architecture of the Gare des Ardoines is inspired by its urban context. The area has been undergoing changes, experiencing a transformation of its industry in recent years. Originally linked to energy and transport, the district is now turning to the health sector and new technologies. This new territory will undergo considerable densification, and the new station is inspired by this context.

The design of the exposed concrete structure is derived from biomorphology. This 'skeleton' takes root deep in the station, at the level of the platforms. From that point, it becomes lighter as it rises, and extending outside to form a footbridge that crosses the rail tracks. It gradually hollows out until it assumes a lacework pattern.

The progression of the forms employed, translated by diamond shapes with rounded angles, allows users to have a sense of their vertical movement. The pattern gradually thickens as it goes down to the platforms and inversely becomes lighter as users moved toward the exterior. This dynamic skeleton finally emerges and creates the volume of the station.

The underground connection between the Grand Paris network and the RER C has been completed with an overhead connection in the footbridge that serves as a belvedere with a view on the developing city of Vitry, situated between the railway tracks and the River Seine.

2025 Vert de Maisons Station (Grand Paris Express Station)

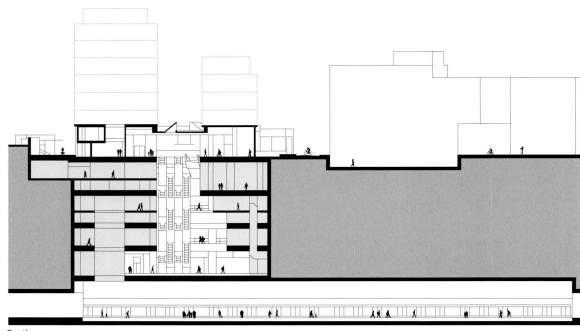

Section

Location Maisons-Alfort / Alfortville, France
Client Société du Grand Paris
Area 75,347 ft² (7,000 m²)
Photography Valode & Pistre

This Grand Paris Express network station, which comes after Maisons-Alfort / Alfortville, opens onto a square lined with shops. It is topped by a new tertiary complex and is connected to the RER C rapid transport line.

The commercial building consists of two elongated parallel structures. They interact with the space in front of them: the first one, in brick, responds to the architecture of the HBM City; the other, aligned along the railway tracks, develops a kinetic and stratified glass and metal façade that plays on the idea of movement and speed. One expresses the integration of the project, the other its new dynamics.

The underground part of the station is imagined as a vast and deep cavity whose section increases with depth. It is treated like a limestone quarry This is a way of evoking the historical activity of Maisons-Alfort, where the stones for many of Paris' monuments were extracted. Between its 'façades,' its 'roofs,' and its 'columns,' finished with reconstituted stone, multiple escalators in steel and glass allow the vertical movement of the public. For the passengers, descent and ascent become a real spatial and aesthetic experience in a unique Piranesian space.

All these architectural and urban devices give a new appeal to the train journey of travelers.

2025 Pont de Rungis Station (Grand Paris Express Station)

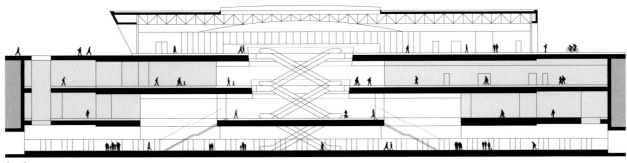
Section

Location Thiais, France
Client Société du Grand Paris
Area 75,347 ft² (7,000 m²)
Photography Valode & Pistre

The Pont de Rungis station on the Grand Paris Express network is located to the north of Orly airport, in an industrial area that is currently being urbanized. The emerging volume of the station is thus designed as the starting point for this new urban development, which will be laid out according to the four cardinal directions.

The interior of the station is designed like a wide path on a ridge with taut lines, which allows daylight to enter deep into the building. The façades of the structure also open out across a large arcade. Natural lighting thus accompanies the movement of the superimposed steel-and-glass escalators that descend to the station platforms. Ascent and descent thus become a real experience for users.

The rib roof of the reception hall evokes the celestial vault because of the quality of the light that is diffused in the interior. The artist Lyes Hammadouche has worked with this aspect of the project, imagining his intervention as a combination of satellite objects and projected images.

2025 Monaco Sea Extension

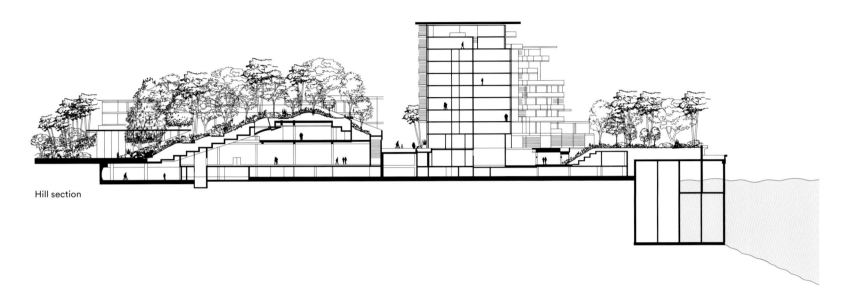

Hill section

Location Monte Carlo, Monaco
Client SAM Anse du Portier
Area 646,000 ft² (60,000 m²) on a 14.8-acre (6-ha) site
Photography Valode & Pistre

Creating an offshore extension is an artificial process. This project design takes the opposite view, giving credit to the idea that this new area reclaimed from the sea is natural. It strives to create two ecosystems, one terrestrial (the extension itself), the other marine (offshore from the extension).

The construction technique for the offshore extension involves building a large seawall made of reinforced concrete coffers. When this protective wall is complete, the infilling operation will be carried out without affecting the nearby seabed. The resulting platform, covering 14.8 acres (6 hectares), has a raised center in the form of a hill, which justifies the new curve of the coastline it wraps around. The new landscape will be planted with a large number of umbrella pines.

The district located on the new extension will be both varied and mixed. Villas will stand along the seafront, reminiscent of early urban development on the Riviera. Under the hill, several exhibition spaces will complement the neighboring Grimaldi Forum.

The southern section will lie around the edge of a small pleasure harbor, a new leisure facility for the principality featuring restaurants and shops. A large residential building on stilts between the harbor and the sea, designed by Renzo Piano, will form the most predominant maritime feature of the development.

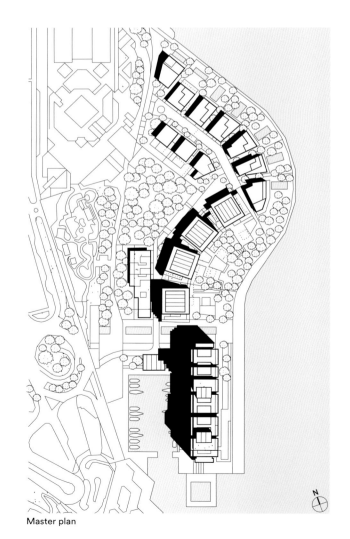

Master plan

(STUDIES) Gare du Nord

South elevation

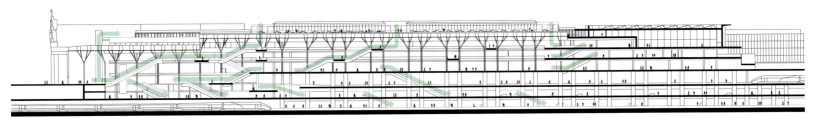

Longitudinal section

Location Paris, France
Client Ceetrus/Gares & Connexions
Area 1,184,030 ft² (110,000 m²)
Photography Valode & Pistre

The ambition of this project is to transform the station into an urban complex, making it a new reference for the twenty-first century. The project is an opportunity to reinvent the overall design of the station and enhance its relationship with the city.

Areas of consideration include the separation of flows between departures and arrivals as well as the redevelopment of the fundamental areas to accommodate the new services and activities. The creation of a main entrance, a large loggia opening onto the forecourt to the east of the historic façade of the station, provides access to a generous 984-foot-long (300-meter-long) passageway beneath a glazed roof. This sunlit gallery spans the length of the new building, guiding users to departure points and serving new commercial, cultural, sporting, and coworking activities. The size of the existing area will be quintupled. The project's objective is to open up the station onto the city. It'll no longer be a station in the city, but a city in the station.

The project highlights the connections between city transport networks and the train station: new bus station, large bike station, and in particular improved access to the Métro. Respect for historical heritage will guide the design. The interior façade of the large hall designed by J. Hittorff in the nineteenth century will be restored to its original state, becoming a landmark greeting point for travelers on the main European lines.

First-floor and circulation plan

258

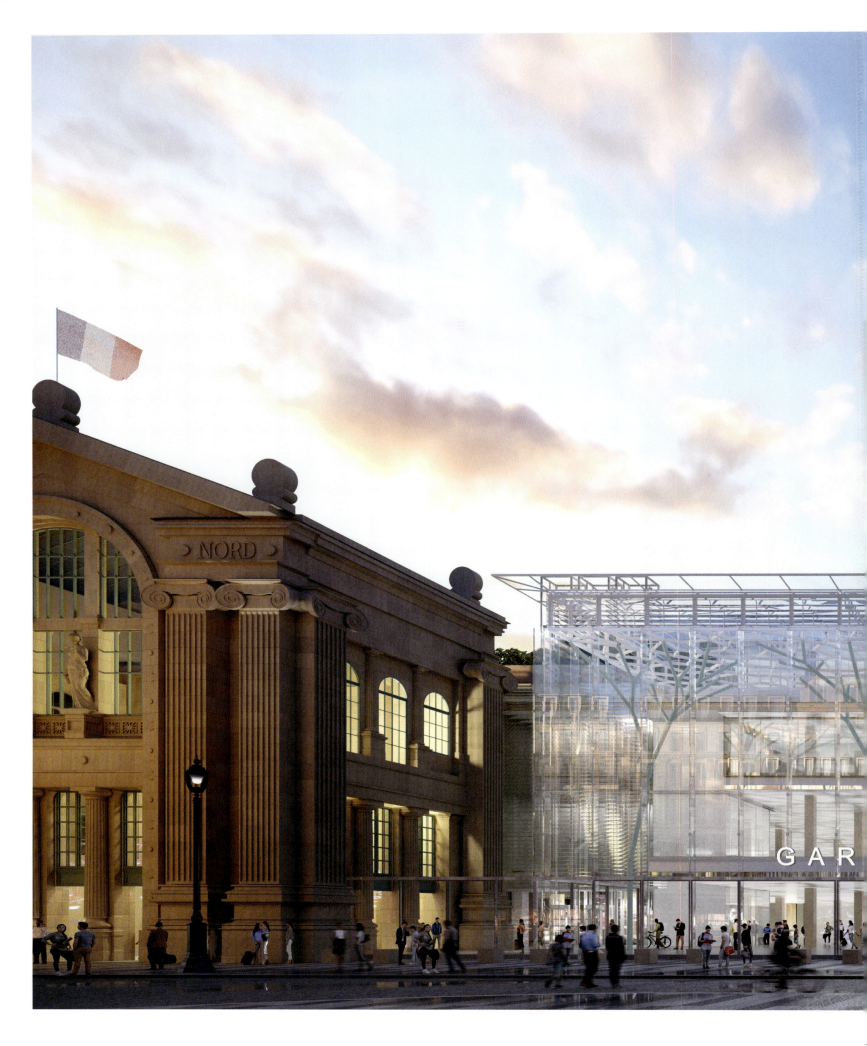

(STUDIES) Jeddah City Mall

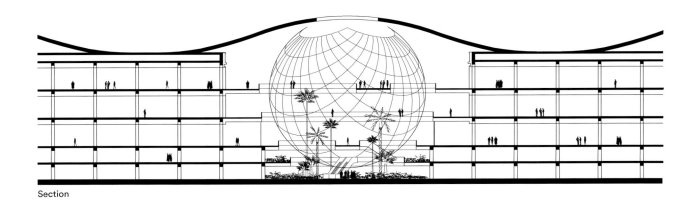
Section

Location Jeddah, Saudi Arabia
Client JEC
Area 10,764,000 ft² (1 million m²)
Photography Valode & Pistre

Jeddah City Mall is a mixed-use project—including shops, offices, a conference center, an exhibition center, restaurants, and leisure facilities—developed at the foot of the world's tallest tower, Jeddah Tower (formerly Kingdom Tower), which is still under construction.

This interaction is materialized in the form of a concentric movement, a ripple that spreads out from the tower that forms its epicenter. The regular waves of the design create multi-arched interior spaces and an undulating outer surface supporting a garden that consists of a series of planted microvalleys.

A regular orthogonal geometric pattern is coordinated with the radial concentric waves. This supports three levels of floors with an arched roof forming a torus. The undulating surface of the roof, cut off at the edge by an inclined plane, forms spacious canopies and highlights the entrances.

Large spherical caps at the top of the waves on the roof form transparent domes over the squares. The height of the staves gradually increases to include office areas under the arches—three towers thus emerge, coordinated with the overall sense of movement.

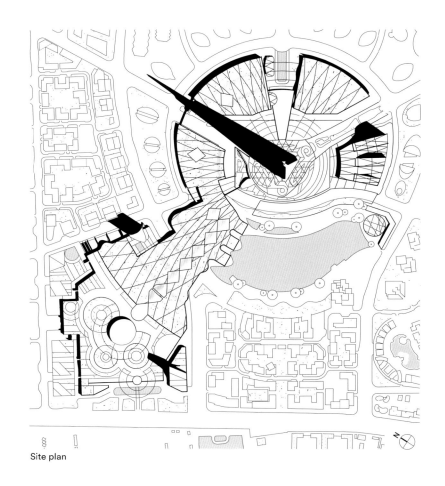
Site plan

Index

A
ABC (Autonomous Building for Citizens) 226–27
Airbus Group Leadership University 176–81
Air France Headquarters 46–47
art, culture, and sport
    CAPC Bordeaux Contemporary Art Museum 26–31
    Cinetic 124–27
    Leonardo da Vinci University 42–45
    Lille Main Stadium 136–39
    Mohammed VI Exhibition Center 166–67
    Paris Convention Centre, Pavilion 7 200–203
    Paris Expo, Pavilion 4 54–55
    Paris Expo, Pavilion 5 84
    Paris Expo, Pavilion 6 216–19
    Shenyang Culture Hub 146–47
    Shenzhen Exhibition Center 210–15
    UGC Ciné-Cité Bercy 56–59
    UGC Ciné-Cité Strasbourg 60–61

B
Beaugrenelle Paris 140–45
Beirut Souks 158–61
Belier Foundry 20–21
Bercy Village 64–69
BioMérieux Headquarters 184–89
Biopark Technology Center 110–13
Bouygues Technopole 128–31
Bretonneau Hospital 62–63
Bulgari Hotel 234–35
Bull Group Research Center 24–25

C
Campus Sanofi 162–65
CAPC Bordeaux Contemporary Art Museum 26–31
Capgemini University 76–79
China
    Shenyang Culture Hub 146–47
    Shenzhen Hospital 204–05
    Shimao Tower 148–49
    Valeo Generic Factories 72
Cinetic 124–27
Clarins Headquarters 156–57
commercial, mixed-use, offices, and retail
    Air France Headquarters 46–47
    Beaugrenelle Paris 140–45
    Beirut Souks 158–61
    Belier Foundry 20–21
    BioMérieux Headquarters 184–89
    Biopark Technology Center 110–13
    Bouygues Technopole 128–31
    Bulgari Hotel 234–35
    Bull Group Research Center 24–25
    Cinetic 124–27
    Clarins Headquarters 156–57
    Crystal Park 94–97
    Havas Advertising Headquarters 90–93
    Hyatt Hotel Yekaterinburg 120–23
    Incity Tower 170–75
    Issy—Cœur de Ville 238–43
    Jeddah City Mall 266–69
    Johnson & Johnson Headquarters 52–53
    L'Ilo 150–51
    L'Oréal Factory 36–41
    L'Oréal Laboratories 106–9
    Montrouge Academy 236–37
    Opus 12 Tower 98–101
    Regional Judiciary Police Department 198–99
    Renault Technocentre, La Ruche 48–51
    Renault Technocentre, Le Gradient 82
    Saint-Gobain Tower 220–25
    Shell Headquarters 32–35
    Shimao Tower 148
    Skolkovo Innovation Center 206–9
    T1 Tower—Engie Headquarters 114–19
    Thomson LGT Factory 22–23
    Transpac 80–81
    Valeo Generic Factories 72–73
    ZB4—The Wilo Building 74–75
Crystal Park 94–97
culture, see art, culture, and sport

D
Damac Tower 182–83

E
education and healthcare
    Airbus Group Leadership University 176–81
    Bretonneau Hospital 62–63
    Campus Sanofi 162–65
    Capgemini University 76–79
    Gonesse Hospital 190–91
    Leonardo da Vinci University 42–45
    Lorient Hospital 132–35
    Shenzhen Hospital 204–5
    University of Toulouse—Jean Jaurès 192–97
    Urban Garden 232–33

F
France
    ABC (Autonomous Building for Citizens) 226–27
    Airbus Group Leadership University 176–81
    Air France Headquarters 46–47
    Beaugrenelle Paris 140–45
    Belier Foundry 20–21
    Bercy Village 64–69
    BioMérieux Headquarters 184–89
    Biopark Technology Center 110–13
    Bouygues Technopole 128–31
    Bretonneau Hospital 62–63
    Bulgari Hotel 234–35
    Bull Group Research Center 24–25
    Campus Sanofi 162–65
    CAPC Bordeaux Contemporary Art Museum 26–31
    Capgemini University 76–79
    Cinetic 124–27
    Clarins Headquarters 156–57
    Crystal Park 94–97
    Gare du Nord 258–65
    Gonesse Hospital 190–91
    Havas Advertising Headquarters 90–93
    Incity Tower 170–75
    Initial Tower 86–89
    Issy—Cœur de Ville 238–43
    Johnson & Johnson Headquarters 52–53
    Laennec Rive Gauche 168–69
    Leonardo da Vinci University 42–45
    Les Ardoines Station (Grand Paris Express Station) 246–47
    Lille Main Stadium 136–39
    L'Ilo 150–51
    L'Oréal Factory 36–41
    L'Oréal Laboratories 106–9
    Lorient Hospital 132–35
    Montrouge Academy 236–37
    Opus 12 Tower 98–101
    Paris Convention Centre, Pavilion 7 200–203
    Paris Expo, Pavilion 4 54–55
    Paris Expo, Pavilion 5 84–85
    Paris Expo, Pavilion 6 216–19
    Pont de Rungis Station (Grand Paris Express Station) 250–51
    Prado Concorde 228–31
    Promenade Sainte-Catherine 152–55
    Regional Judiciary Police Department 198–99
    Renault Technocentre, La Ruche 48–51
    Renault Technocentre, Le Gradient 82–83

Saint-Gobain Tower 220–25
Shell Headquarters 32–35
Shenzhen Exhibition Center 210–15
T1 Tower—Engie Headquarters 114–19
Thomson LGT Factory 22–23
Transpac 80–81
Triangle de l'Arche 70–71
UGC Ciné-Cité Bercy 56–59
UGC Ciné-Cité Strasbourg 60–61
University of Toulouse—Jean Jaurès 192–97
Urban Garden 232–33
Vert de Maisons Station (Grand Paris Express Station) 248–49
ZB4—The Wilo Building 74–75

G
Gare du Nord 258–65
Gonesse Hospital 190–91

H
Havas Advertising Headquarters 90–93
healthcare, see education and healthcare
Hendrikhof Tilburg 244–45
Hungary
    Valeo Generic Factories 72–73
Hyatt Hotel Yekaterinburg 120–23

I
Incity Tower 170–75
Initial Tower 86–89
interior design
    Clarins Headquarters 156–57
    Gare du Nord 258–65
    Hyatt Hotel Yekaterinburg 120–23
    Incity Tower 170–75
    Initial Tower 86–89
Issy—Cœur de Ville 238–43

J
Jeddah City Mall 266–69
Johnson & Johnson Headquarters 52–53

L
Laennec Rive Gauche 168–69
Las Mercedes 102–5
Lebanon
    Beirut Souks 158–61
    Damac Tower 182–83
Leonardo da Vinci University 42–45
Les Ardoines Station (Grand Paris Express Station) 246–47
Lille Main Stadium 136–39
L'Ilo 150–51
L'Oréal Factory 36–41
L'Oréal Laboratories 106–9
Lorient Hospital 132–35

M
Mexico
    Valeo Generic Factories 72–73
mixed-use, see commercial, mixed-use, offices, and retail
Mohammed VI Exhibition Center 166–67
Monaco Sea Extension 252–57
Montrouge Academy 236–37
Morocco
    Mohammed VI Exhibition Center 166–67
    Valeo Generic Factories 72–73

N
The Netherlands
    Hendrikhof Tilburg 244–45

O
offices, see commercial, mixed-use, offices, and retail
Opus 12 Tower 98–101

P
Paris Convention Centre, Pavilion 7 200–203
Paris Expo, Pavilion 4 54–55
Paris Expo, Pavilion 5 84–85
Paris Expo, Pavilion 6 216–19
Pont de Rungis Station (Grand Paris Express Station) 250–51
Prado Concorde 228–31
Promenade Sainte-Catherine 152–55

R
Regional Judiciary Police Department 198–99
Renault Technocentre, La Ruche 48–51
Renault Technocentre, Le Gradient 82–83
residential
    ABC (Autonomous Building for Citizens) 226–27
    Damac Tower 182–83
    Hyatt Hotel Yekaterinburg 120–23
    Laennec Rive Gauche 168–69
retail, see commercial, mixed-use, offices, and retail
Russia
    Hyatt Hotel Yekaterinburg 120–23
    Skolkovo Innovation Center 206–9

S
Saint-Gobain Tower 220–25
Saudi Arabia
    Jeddah City Mall 266–69
Shell Headquarters 32–35
Shenyang Culture Hub 146–47
Shenzhen Exhibition Center 210–15
Shenzhen Hospital 204–5
Shimao Tower 148–49
Skolkovo Innovation Center 206–9
Spain
    Las Mercedes 102–05
sport, see art, culture, and sport

T
T1 Tower—Engie Headquarters 114–19
Thomson LGT Factory 22–23
Transpac 80–81
transportation, see urban planning and transportation
Triangle de l'Arche 70–71

U
UGC Ciné-Cité Bercy 56–59
UGC Ciné-Cité Strasbourg 60–61
University of Toulouse—Jean Jaurès 192–97
Urban Garden 232–33
urban planning and transportation
    Bercy Village 64–69
    Gare du Nord 258–65
    Hendrikhof Tilburg 244–45
    Issy—Cœur de Ville 238–43
    Jeddah City Mall 266–69
    Las Mercedes 102–5
    Les Ardoines Station (Grand Paris Express Station) 246–47
    Monaco Sea Extension 252–57
    Pont de Rungis Station (Grand Paris Express Station) 250–51
    Prado Concorde 228–31
    Promenade Sainte-Catherine 152–55
    Triangle de l'Arche 70–71
    Vert de Maisons Station (Grand Paris Express Station) 248–49

V
Valeo Generic Factories 72–73
Vert de Maisons Station (Grand Paris Express Station) 248–49

Z
ZB4—The Wilo Building 74–75

Published in Australia in 2022 by
The Images Publishing Group Pty Ltd
ABN 89 059 734 431

Offices

Melbourne
Waterman Business Centre
Suite 64, Level 2 UL40
1341 Dandenong Road
Chadstone, Victoria 3148
Australia
Tel: +61 3 8564 8122

New York
6 West 18th Street 4B
New York City, NY 10011
United States
Tel: +1 212 645 1111

Shanghai
6F, Building C, 838 Guangji Road
Hongkou District, Shanghai 200434
China
Tel: +86 021 31260822

books@imagespublishing.com
www.imagespublishing.com

Copyright © Philip Jodidio (text); photographer/s as indicated 2022
The Images Publishing Group Reference Number: 1291

All photography is attributed with the individual projects, with the following exceptions:
Office of Valode & Pistre—Pages 4, 16: Philippe Chancel; pages 9–15: Jared Chulski

All rights reserved. Apart from any fair dealing for the purposes of private study, research, criticism or review as permitted under the Copyright Act, no part of this publication may be reproduced, stored in a retrieval system, or transmitted in any form by any means, electronic, mechanical, photocopying, recording or otherwise, without the written permission of the publisher.

 A catalogue record for this book is available from the National Library of Australia

Title: Valode & Pistre: Complete Works: 1980 to Present // Philip Jodidio
ISBN: 9781864707151

This title was commissioned in IMAGES' Melbourne office and produced as follows:
Editorial Georgia (Gina) Tsarouhas, Bree de Roche, *Graphic design* Ryan Marshall, *Production* Nicole Boehringer
With thanks to Jordan El Ouardi (Valode & Pistre) for the layouts.

Printed by Graphius nv, Belgium, on 150gsm matte coated FSC art paper

IMAGES has included on its website a page for special notices in relation to this and its other publications. Please visit www.imagespublishing.com

Every effort has been made to trace the original source of copyright material contained in this book. The publishers would be pleased to hear from copyright holders to rectify any errors or omissions.

The information and illustrations in this publication have been prepared and supplied by Valode & Pistre and Philip Jodidio. While all reasonable efforts have been made to ensure accuracy, the publishers do not, under any circumstances, accept responsibility for errors, omissions and representations express or implied.